WITNESS

WITNESS

Highlights from
The Wiener Holocaust Library Collections

**The Wiener
Holocaust Library**

First published July 2023 by Stephen Morris for
The Wiener Holocaust Library

© Foreword Hartwig Fischer; Introduction Barbara Warnock

ISBN 978 1 7396050 5 6

British Library Cataloguing-in-Publication Data
A catalogue record for this book is available from the British Library

All rights reserved. Except for the purpose of review, no part of this book
may be reproduced, stored in a retrieval system, or transmitted, in any
form or by any means, electronic, mechanical, photocopying, recording or
otherwise, without the prior permission of the publishers.

www.stephen-morris.co.uk

STEPHEN MORRIS

The Wiener Holocaust Library
29 Russell Square
London WC1B 5DP

Contents

Foreword: Hartwig Fischer

No one
bears witness for the
witness

Paul Celan, 'Ashglory', *Breathturn*, 1967

The fifty documents presented in this book – letters, journals, drawings, photographs, testimonies, reports, publications – are related to the crime of genocide, the destruction of the Jews in Europe and the territories occupied by Nazi Germany. Reaching back as far as the eighteenth century they focus on the history of antisemitism after 1900, the gradual isolation and spoliation of the Jewish population in Germany and the territories occupied by Germany between 1933 and 1945. They bear witness to the systematic murder by killing squads and in death and concentration camps after the beginning of the Second World War. They speak of intolerable suffering, despair and loss, families destroyed, children orphaned, the fabric of human relations ripped apart, the millions who perished or were traumatised. They speak of the perpetrators and collaborators. And they speak of courage, resilience, rescue, and humanity, not least in the United Kingdom, in the face of cruelty and violence.

The fifty documents presented in this book reveal the determination of Alfred Wiener and his colleagues to counter antisemitism since the early 1920s, warn of its destructiveness, document the injustices and crimes committed against Jews after the Nazis came to power, support individuals trying to escape annihilation, convince governments and organisations to act and remind them of their obligation to protect, identify and commemorate the victims, research the atrocities, help bring the criminals to justice, and in doing so create – alongside the United States Holocaust Memorial Museum Library and Archives in Washington DC and Yad Vashem in Jerusalem – one of the world's most important centres for the study of the Holocaust.

The majority of the fifty documents assembled in this book pertain to Jewish individuals and communities, before, during and after the Holocaust. Others concern the perpetrators, the ideologues, organisers and executors, in Germany and in other countries. Again other documents allow us to understand the extraordinary achievement of Wiener and those who worked with him in Berlin, Amsterdam and London, as activists against racism, witnesses, archivists, and documentalists. But also of their personal losses: Wiener's wife, Margarete Wiener, who had been deported to Bergen-Belsen camp, died immediately after her release.

A few items also highlight the genocide directed against minorities like the Roma, or in other regions preceding the Holocaust, such as in the case of the Armenians of the Ottoman empire, or more recently in Darfur, Sudan.

As different as these documents are, some are handwritten, some mass produced, many are texts, others are images preserving the traits of men, women and children, some are intimate traces of individual lives, some are destined for public use, they all speak with haunting insistence and precision. Take the so-called 'Motorcycle Album' (page 29), which documents how antisemitic acts of exclusion had permeated the remotest villages across Germany by 1935, or Gerda Nabe's schoolwork (page 33), which shows us how the Nazis instilled their racist ideologies in the mind of children. And the record card (page 51) with details of a twelve-year-old, Julius Blumenthal from Frankfurt, who sought refuge in Britain. The card is part of the institutional records of a small charitable organisation set up to try to help children who sought to come to Britain on the *Kindertransport* scheme. The Red Cross telegram by Franz Kuhn (page 71), was a precious opportunity to communicate to family or friends outside the zone of persecution and destruction. The map of the Stahlecker Report of October 1941 (page 65), proudly documenting the systematic 'Jewish Executions Carried Out by *Einsatzgruppe A*', months before the Wannsee conference, or the photograph of German soldiers filming the Pogrom of Lvov in June and July 1941 (page 63), are documents that corroborate the testimonies of those who survived and bore witness. The International Tracing Service's map showing the grave of Sergii Posnik (page 89), killed on one of the forced marches of concentration camp prisoners, is a testament to the effort to identify those who perished in the Holocaust. There is the photograph of the 'Boys' arriving in Windermere in 1945 disembarking from a plane (page 91) after the British government had granted asylum to 1,000 child survivors of the Holocaust. And Rachel Auerbach's 1947 report on the extermination camp of Treblinka (page 93), an important contribution to establishing the facts of the Holocaust after 1945.

This publication with fifty documents from The Wiener Holocaust Library is itself an important contribution to our knowledge of the Holocaust, pertinent knowledge, necessary knowledge. Knowledge that reminds us of our responsibility as human beings.

Introduction: Barbara Warnock

The World's Oldest Archive on the Nazi Era and the Holocaust

In 1933 in Amsterdam, Alfred Wiener, a German Jew living in exile from Nazism, and David Cohen, co-founder of a Dutch committee established to support Jewish refugees fleeing Nazi Germany, formulated an idea to create an organisation to monitor and challenge the Nazi regime. Later that year, at an international conference of Jewish groups held in London, Cohen obtained backing for the creation of a body to gather and distribute intelligence relating to the Nazis.

Named the Jewish Central Information Office (JCIO), with Cohen as President and Wiener as Director, the organisation started work in Amsterdam on 1 February 1934. Throughout the rest of the 1930s, the JCIO created what was then the most extensive repository of knowledge and evidence about the Nazi movement and the position of Jews in Nazi Germany in the world. The documents gathered and reports produced by the JCIO still today provide us with a crucial body of contemporary documents about the increasingly systematic persecution and murder of civilians by the Nazis on racial and political grounds, as well as illuminating evidence about the methods and tactics of those working to challenge and raise awareness about the Nazi and fascist threat.

The JCIO shares a continuous history with The Wiener Holocaust Library, which today is based in Russell Square in central London. The archive moved to London in 1939, as Alfred Wiener encountered increasing concern from the Dutch government about the organisation's activities. Wiener obtained permission to relocate the JCIO to Britain, and a large proportion of its documents were shipped to London, where the JCIO opened its office on 1 September 1939.

During the Second World War, the JCIO worked closely with the British government to supply intelligence on the Nazi regime, and it came to be known as 'Dr Wiener's Library'. Following the defeat of Germany, the Library's focus changed from engagement in the active fight against Nazism to ensuring that the crimes of the Nazis and their collaborators were documented and remembered for the historical record.

This book, created to mark the ninetieth anniversary of the foundation of the JCIO, highlights a selection of the Library's collections with a view to telling the story of the archive and its construction, as well as the histories of some of the documents and objects within, items that testify to the experiences and actions of victims and perpetrators of the Holocaust, and other eyewitnesses.

The Library holds rare documentation on a wide range of subjects relating to Nazi persecution and the Holocaust. Among its earliest holdings are documents on the early struggles against antisemitism and Nazism conducted by Alfred Wiener and others in Germany before the Nazi accession to power (page 13). The Library also has photographs, personal and official documentation that illuminate the lives of Jews and other victims of Nazi persecution before the Nazi era (page 25). The JCIO's efforts to record and disseminate evidence of Nazi oppression in the 1930s are seen in some of the Library's most important collections, including eyewitness accounts of *Kristallnacht* from 1938-1939 (page 45), which are a vital record of this brutal escalation of Nazi anti-Jewish measures.

The documents featured in this book also attest to the contribution that the Library's staff made to the process of documenting the atrocities of the Nazis and their collaborators, and to the developing field of Holocaust research. In 1942, the Library publicised evidence about the operation of Auschwitz as a killing centre in its English-language publication *Jewish News* (page 69). In 1945, the Library was the recipient and publisher of some of the earliest survivor accounts of the camp (page 87), and in the 1950s, the Library's Director of Research led a project to gather early witness accounts of the Holocaust from across Europe (page 99).

The Library and its archive have their roots in German and Austrian refugee communities in Britain, and this has shaped the nature of the historical record that the Library's collections form. Thus, the substantial collections relating to the lives and experiences of Jewish refugees in Britain that have been gathered in recent decades are generally records relating to refugees from these countries. This volume contains, for example, a photograph of the Simon family in Berlin (page 23), and the remarkable set of diaries and journals maintained in the Theresienstadt camp and ghetto by Philipp Manes, a German Jew (page 77).

The Library also has important documents relating to the Nazi genocide against Europe's Roma, including rare survivor accounts from the 1950s (page 105), and documentation from the first effort to comprehensively research the genocide, a project that the Library supported. In recent decades, we have received material relating to other genocides, most notably that in Darfur (page 109), and also substantial digital archives, such as a copy of the International Tracing Service digital archive: an enormous collection of Nazi and other documents used since the end of the Second World War to trace the fates of the lost and the missing of the Second World War (pages 85 and 89).

The importance of the Library's collections is attested to by the rarity of some of the items contained within it: Wolf Zappert's 1774 conveyance (page 11); and a document signed by Raoul Wallenberg, a Swedish diplomat, that helped a whole family to survive the war and the Holocaust (page 83). And the fragility of some of these documents – such as Charlotte and Richard Holzer's account of their resistance activities in Berlin during the war (page 103) – emphasises the importance of the Library's work in conserving such evidence for future generations.

Today, the Library continues to build upon its collections and seeks to enhance public knowledge and understanding of the Nazi era, the Holocaust, and other genocides, using its unique and precious historical collections, documents into which this book provides an insight.

... Comißarij ...

... Prag den ... Martij 1774

Cantzler ... Pilgram ...
Comißarius

Johann ...
Comißarius

... Jacob ...

... 1774 ...

Conveyance of the first Jewish house bought outside the ghetto, Prague, 1774

Wolf Zappert's conveyance is the oldest document in the Library's collections. In 2012, it was donated to the Library by Zappert's great-great-great-great granddaughter, Marianne Maxwell, a Jewish refugee from Nazism who came to Britain in 1939.

Wolf Zappert (d. 1810) was a successful jeweller and well-known philanthropist in Prague. Zappert asked the Holy Roman Emperor for permission to establish a house outside the Jewish ghetto in order to conduct his business more efficiently. The Emperor agreed, and Zappert became the first Jew in Prague to live outside the ghetto.

Zappert's document reveals the improving social position of some Jews in late eighteenth-century Europe. Preserved by the family for over two hundred years, it is one of a number of documents that reflect the Zappert family history, as well as aspects of the history of Jews in central Europe. The Zappert collection includes title deeds and other documents relating to the purchase and sale of properties, last wills and testaments, registration records and marriage contracts.

By 1938, the Zappert family lived in Vienna, where Wolf Zappert's great-great grandson Julius Zappert (1867-1941) was a paediatrician and university professor who was imprisoned by the Nazis after their takeover of Austria. Marianne Maxwell came to Britain with her parents as a refugee from Nazism in 1939, as did Julius, her grandfather.

Wolf Zappert's conveyancing document was transported from central Europe to Britain as a result of the Nazi persecution of Jews in Austria. Its journey to The Wiener Holocaust Library in London reflects the displacement of Jews from central Europe, and the eradication of much of Jewish culture there during the Nazi era.

Vorpo-
gromen
?

Alfred Wiener: *Vor Pogrommen* (*Prelude to Pogroms* or *Before Pogroms*), 1919

This pamphlet, published in Germany shortly after the First World War, is an important early document in The Wiener Holocaust Library collections. It reveals the concerns that the Library's founder, Dr Alfred Wiener (1885-1964), had about the activities of antisemitic groups in Germany at this time. This was Wiener's first publication, written shortly after he had been demobilised from the German army.

In the aftermath of the First World War, Germany faced the humiliation of defeat and an enforced peace treaty, as well as political instability, polarisation and social and economic difficulties. Antisemitic myths, such as the idea that Germany's Jews had betrayed their country and sought its defeat, were propagated in nationalist militaristic circles and gained some traction amongst the wider German public. This notion of Jewish betrayal drew heavily on antisemitic nineteenth-century German nationalist ideas in which Jews were portrayed as a foreign, malevolent influence working to deliberately undermine Germany.

Alfred Wiener's perception of the dangers inherent in the rising levels of antisemitism in Germany was acute. In this pamphlet, he analysed antisemitic groups, their sources of funding and connections, and warned that antisemitism in Germany might eventually result in violent attacks on Jews in Germany.

AN DIE DEUTSCHEN MÜTTER!

72000 jüdische Soldaten sind für das Vaterland auf dem Felde der Ehre gefallen.

Christliche und jüdische Helden haben gemeinsam gekämpft und ruhen gemeinsam in fremder Erde.

12000 Juden fielen im Kampf!

Blindwütiger Parteihaß macht vor den Gräbern der Toten nicht Halt.

Deutsche Frauen,

duldet nicht, daß die jüdische Mutter in ihrem Schmerz verhöhnt wird.

Reichsbund jüdischer Frontsoldaten E. V.

Lindemann u. Lüdecke, Berlin O.18.

Poster produced by the *Reichsbund jüdischer Frontsoldaten* (Association of Jewish Soldiers), 1920

The Association of Jewish Soldiers was an organisation of Jewish war veterans founded in 1919 in Germany to counter accusations that Jews were unpatriotic or had not contributed to the German war effort.

In the aftermath of Germany's defeat in the First World War, German nationalist groups such as the *Alldeutschen Verband* (Pan-German Association) flourished. They promoted the idea that Jews weren't true Germans, and promulgated antisemitic myths that claimed that Jews had shirked their duty or had even caused the defeat of Germany.

The Association of Jewish Soldiers produced this poster to remind people of the service and sacrifice of German Jews. The top section of the text reads:

> *To the German Mother! 12,000 Jewish soldiers fell for the Fatherland in the field of honour: Christian and Jewish heroes fought together and rest together in foreign soil'*

It goes on to urge German women not to allow Jewish mothers' grief to be overlooked.

An estimated 100,000 Jewish soldiers fought in the German Army in the First World War, of whom 12,000 perished. The founder of The Wiener Library, Alfred Wiener, like many German-Jewish soldiers, was awarded an Iron Cross for his brave service during the War.

Ronnie and Beryl Roberts and their cousins in Wiesbaden, *c.*1920s

This photograph comes from a collection donated to the Library by Carol Roberts, wife of Ronald (Ronnie) Roberts (1921-2001), after his death. Roberts was born in Wiesbaden in Germany to a white German mother and a British/Barbadian father. Roberts experienced racist persecution at the hands of the Nazis during the 1930s and was interned as a British national in German camps during the Second World War. After working for the British army of occupation and running a bar in Vienna, Ronnie settled in Britain in the early 1950s. He later married Carol and ran a hotel in Devon.

This photograph depicts Ronnie and his sister Beryl as children with their cousins. The Roberts family experienced racism during this period as a result of being a mixed heritage family, and this intensified during the Nazi era. The Nuremberg Laws targeted Black people as well as Jews and Roma. Thus some 20,000 Black Germans were both rendered stateless and prohibited from forming relationships with 'Aryan' Germans.

At thirteen, Ronnie Roberts was removed from his school on racial grounds and eventually forced by the authorities to work on *Autobahn* (motorway) construction. Aged fifteen, Roberts was told by the Gestapo to report to a hospital. He did not go and in his memoir, also held by the Library, he recounts learning that the authorities were sterilising Black German men.

Ronnie Roberts spent a period in hiding and also applied for a British passport, to which he was eligible through his father. This meant that during the war, Roberts was interned in Germany as a British citizen.

Der Anti-Nazi

Redner- und Pressematerial über die N.S.D.A.P.

...erte Auflage

...ksgemeinschaftsdienst Berlin SW 48

Anti-Anti

Tatsachen zur Judenfrage

7. erweiterte und neu bearbeitete Auflage
29. bis 33. Tausend

Herausgegeben und verlegt vom Centralverein deutscher Staatsbürger jüd. Glaubens E.V. Berlin
Zu beziehen durch: Philo Verlag, Berlin W 15, Emser Straße 42

Innen- und Rückseite beachten!

Anti-Anti: Tatsachen zur Judenfrage and Der Anti-Nazi: Redner und Pressematerial über die N.S.D.A.P ('Facts about the Jewish Question' and 'The Anti-Nazi: Speeches and Press Material about the N.S.D.A.P'), 1930 and 1932

These documents were distributed by staff at Büro Wilhelmstrasse, a small semi-clandestine organisation established in Berlin in 1928 to gather evidence about Nazi Party activities and produce material to analyse and counter antisemitic arguments and the ideas and policies of the Nazis. In the 1920s, Alfred Wiener worked for the Central Association of German Jews (*Centralverein deutscher Staatsbürger jüdischen Glaubens* – CV) in Berlin, an organisation that supported German Jews and tried to combat the idea that German Jews were not fully German. From 1928, the organisation covertly supported the establishment of a small office, Büro Wilhelmstrasse, set up to document Nazi activities and publish anti-Nazi material and refutations of antisemitic arguments.

The Büro published *Anti-Anti*, a collection of leaflets containing facts and arguments to help those who sought to refute Nazi claims and antisemitic propaganda in speeches or in the press. Later the Büro's propagandist and archivist Walter Gyssling (1903-1980) wrote *Der Anti-Nazi*, which focussed on providing information about and critiquing Nazi politicians and policies. Büro Wilhelmstrasse concealed their involvement in the publication of *Anti-Anti* and *Der Anti-Nazi* by inventing a name for a publishing company that appeared to have produced the document.

The first edition of *Der Anti-Nazi* had a print run of 180,000 copies and was just over 30 pages long. By the time that this version was printed in 1932, it ran to 180 pages.

Alfred Wiener was influenced by some of the Büro's organisation and methods when he set up his own organisation in Amsterdam to monitor antisemitism in Germany from 1933.

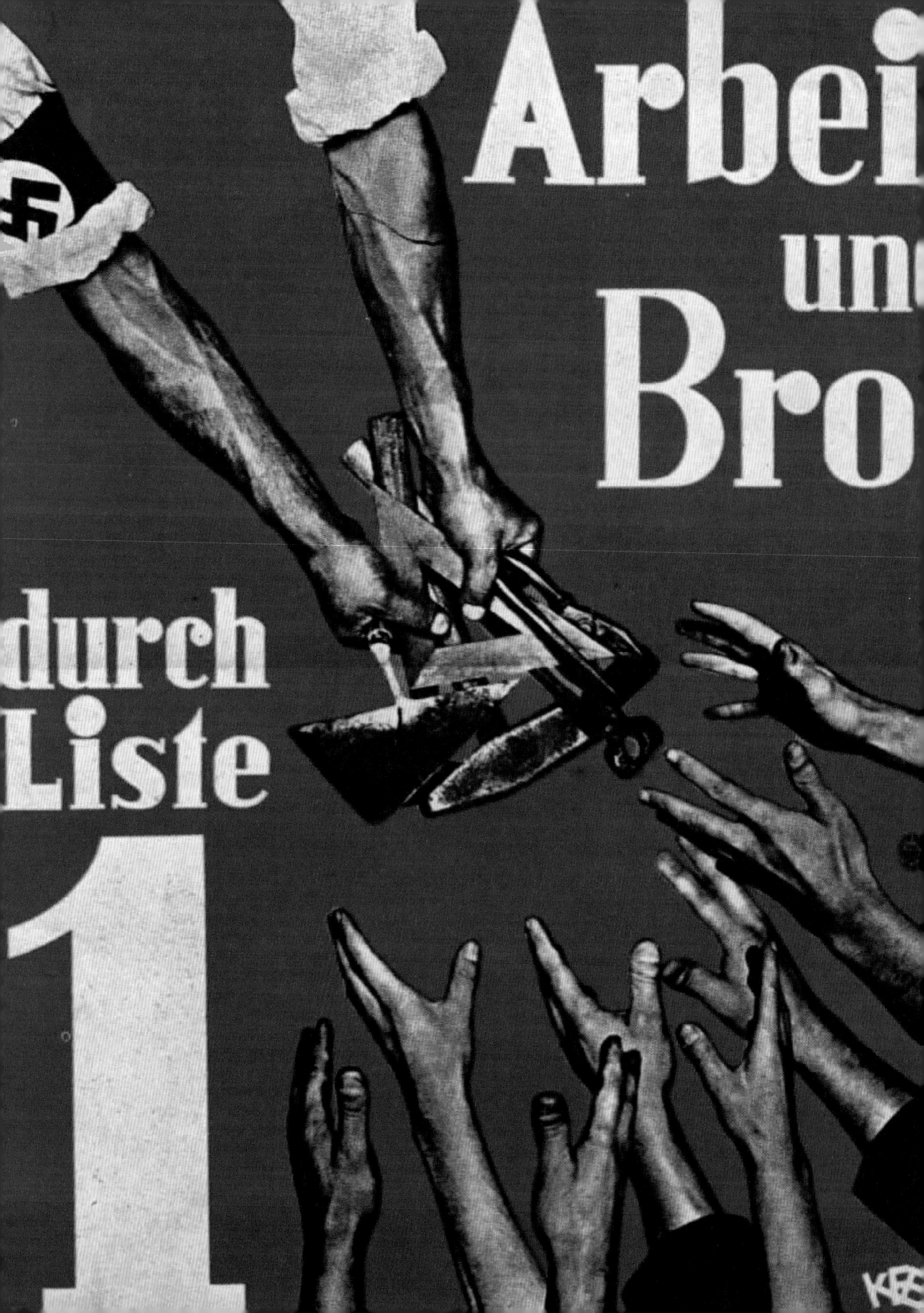
Arbei
un
Bro
durch
Liste
1

Arbeit und Brot ('Work and Bread'), Nazi election poster, 1932

This poster reflects the efforts made by the Nazi Party to appeal to working-class voters in Germany, and the ways in which they exploited the economic depression in Germany to gain support. The poster features iconography that is reminiscent of that of communist parties at the time, and the slogan promises that the Nazis will provide people with work. Germany was the country most badly affected by the Great Depression and, by 1932, its economy had shrunk by 40%. Six million Germans out of a total population of about 60 million were unemployed.

In the course of its work, Büro Wilhelmstrasse amassed a collection of documents relating to Nazi activities and propaganda, and collections of material on election campaigns in Germany. It is possible that this Nazi poster from the Reichstag (parliamentary) election of 1932 comes from the original Büro Wilhelmstrasse collection. However, most of the collection was destroyed in 1933 around the time the Nazis shut the organisation, so it may have entered The Wiener Holocaust Library's collections at a later date.

Gerty Simon: The Simon family: Wilhelm, Bernd (Bernard) and Gerty (Gertrud) in Berlin, early 1930s

The Simons lived in Charlottenburg in Berlin. Gerty Simon (née Cohn, 1887-1970) was a professional photographer who staged a number of successful exhibitions of portraiture in 1929 and 1930. Wilhelm Simon (1885-1966) was a lawyer and a judge who also worked in an official capacity for the German government as part of the Reparations Commission. The position of the Simon family reflected that of many Jews in Germany: they were well connected and deeply rooted in German culture and society.

In 1933, Gerty Simon and her son Bernd (later Bernard, 1921-2015) became some of the earliest Jewish refugees from Nazism. Mother and son relocated with the predominately Jewish staff and students of Bernd's progressive school, which had been based in Ulm. After the Nazi boycott of Jewish businesses on 1 April 1933, headteacher Anna Essinger felt that 'Germany was no longer a place in which to bring up children in honesty and freedom', and she took steps to move her school.

By the autumn of 1933, Essinger had permission from the British authorities to bring the school to Britain, and Gerty Simon moved along with the school, explaining later that

> *under the Nazi regime I found myself as a Jew in particular danger, because as a photographer, I had taken numerous photographs of Social Democratic and anti-fascist personalities and exhibited them in public.*

Wilhelm Simon did not join his wife and son in exile until 1939.

This photograph was deposited in the Library's collections in 2016, after Bernard Simon's death, along with an important collection of Gerty Simon's original photographic prints and other documents relating to the family's experiences as refugees.

From left, Margarete and Alfred Wiener

Staff of the Jewish Central Information Office Amsterdam, *c.*1930s

By the time that the Nazi Party came to power in January 1933, Alfred Wiener was known as an anti-Nazi campaigner. Wiener risked arrest as the Nazis and their supporters moved to eliminate their political enemies from February 1933.

Told by Hermann Goering that he was not welcome in Germany, Wiener relocated to Amsterdam with his wife, Dr Margarete Wiener (1895-1945) and their three daughters. There, he founded his own organisation, the Jewish Central Information Office (JCIO), which opened in February 1934. The JCIO used a network of contacts in Germany to gather evidence and information about the Nazi regime and the position of Jews in Nazi Germany.

The organisation first operated from a hotel room. Later, supported by the Board of Deputies of British Jews amongst others, it was later able to employ a small staff, photographed here outside the JCIO office in Jan van Eijckstraat in Amsterdam. Most of the staff were Jewish exiles from Germany.

FRANZ WERFEL

DIE VIERZIG TAGE DES MUSA DAGH

ROMAN

1. BAND

Franz Werfel: *The Forty Days of Musa Dagh*, 1934

Originally published in Germany in 1933, this novel by Austrian novelist, playwright and poet Franz Werfel (1890-1945), has been credited with awakening the world to the genocide inflicted on the Armenian nation during the First World War. Many contemporaries saw parallels between the events described in the book and the rise of Adolf Hitler and the Nazi Party in the early 1930s. After the *Anschluss* (the German annexation of Austria in 1938), Werfel fled to the United States via France and Portugal.

The Armenian Genocide was the mass murder of at least 664,000 and up to 1.2 million Armenians by the nationalist ruling party of the Ottoman Empire, the Committee of Union and Progress (CUP, also known as the Young Turks), between 1915 and 1916.

During the First World War, the Ottoman Empire joined forces with Germany and Austria-Hungary but suffered several significant defeats and quickly retreated. To conceal their failure from the public, the Ottoman leaders openly blamed their defeat on Armenians in the region and stated that they had betrayed their empire by fighting for and helping the enemy forces. This deliberate falsehood acted as a catalyst and justification for the genocide of the Armenian people.

Armenian soldiers were categorised as a direct threat to the Ottoman war effort, removed from the Ottoman army, and massacred. The intellectual elite of Armenian society, concentrated in areas such as Constantinople, were also rounded up, imprisoned and later murdered. The remaining Armenians, primarily women, the elderly and children, were relocated from strategically important areas and forcibly marched to remote camps by Ottoman forces and local collaborators. Little to no food and water was provided on these 'death marches' – despite the length of the journey – and those who could not keep up or continue were executed. As a result, thousands died.

Some Armenians in low-density areas were able to escape execution by converting to Islam. Young girls and women were also occasionally spared for forced labour as domestic servants, to become wives in Muslim households or to be used as sex slaves.

Those who survived the death marches were imprisoned in camps, where conditions were extremely poor and many thousands died of disease and malnutrition. Between March and October 1916, there was another wave of executions, and as many as 200,000 more people were murdered.

In Heisede
sind Juden
ungebetene Gäste

The 'Motorcycle Album', 1935

A number of copies of this photograph album were produced for The Wiener Holocaust Library's predecessor organisation, the Jewish Central Information Office (JCIO), and they still form an important part of the Library's collection.

In 1935, German-Jewish businessman Werner 'Fritz' Fürstenberg (1903-1971), his fiancée Käthe Smoszewski (1913-2003) and their dog made a journey from the Dutch border of Germany to Berlin in their car. The purpose of the trip was to record every antisemitic street sign that they encountered. The couple photographed signs in towns, villages and cities, on streets and street corners, on the top of a bridge, on front doors and in notice boards. The slogans on the signs included, 'Jews not wanted here', 'Jews are unwelcome guests' and 'Jews are our misfortune and should live away from us'. The signs were varied and sometimes handmade, and did not often feature the Nazi Party's swastika symbol. This may suggest that the signs were erected as a result of local or individual initiatives, and not as part of any systematic Nazi Party policy. The sign pictured here is from Heisede, a village in Lower Saxony. It says 'Jews are not welcome'.

The photographs were passed to the JCIO in Amsterdam, who claimed that they were taken by a Dutch motorcyclist in order to protect Fürstenberg's identity.

Multiple copies of this album were made by the JCIO, and the photographs were also shown in slide shows at talks at the organisation's office in Amsterdam in 1935 and 1936.

The collecting of the photographs was part of the efforts of the JCIO to gather evidence about antisemitism in Germany and during the Nazi regime.

Reichstag für Freiheit und Frieden
Wahlkreis Hessen-Nassau

Nationalsozialistische Deutsche Arbeiterpartei

Adolf Hitler

Heß Frick Göring Goebbels Sprenger Weinrich

A ballot paper from the Reichstag elections, 1936

This ballot paper for the 29 March 1936 Reichstag (parliamentary) election may have been sent to the JCIO from one of its contacts in Germany: it forms part of a collection of documents held by The Wiener Holocaust Library whose provenance is unclear.

The ballot paper is for the constituency of Hessen-Nassau in western Germany. Voters only had one option: to vote for the list of candidates of the National Socialist German Workers Party (Nazi Party), headed by Adolf Hitler. The slogan at the top of the ballot reads: *Reichstag for Freedom and Peace.*

The Nazi Party claimed that the turnout for this election was 99%, and that 98.8% of those who participated in the election selected the Nazi list of candidates. The election also included a referendum asking voters to approve the German remilitarisation of the Rhineland, which the Nazis claimed the German public voted overwhelmingly to support.

By 1936, ballots in Germany did not take place in secret, and voters would have encountered the intimidating presence of members of the SS and SA at polling stations, where Nazi insignia, slogans and portraits of Hitler were displayed.

The ballot paper is evidence of the ways in which the Nazis eliminated democracy whilst maintaining superficially democratic mechanisms to create a sense that the Party, and its policies, had vast popular support.

Erläuterung
zum Reichsbürgergesetz

I

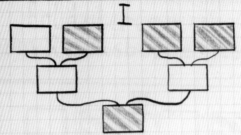

Wer von mindestens 3 der Rasse nach
volljüdischer Grosseltern abstammt,
ist ein Jude.

II

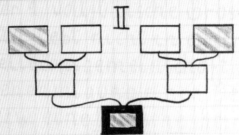

Wer 2 volljüdische Grosseltern hat, ist
ein jüdischer Mischling.
Er ist aber <u>Jude</u>, wenn er einer
jüdischen Religionsgemeinschaft
angehört oder einen <u>Juden</u>
heiratet.

Deutscher ☐  ▨ Jude

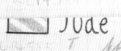

Gerda Nabe: schoolwork, *c.*1935-1936

This diagram forms part of project work produced by German schoolgirl Gerda Nabe in the mid-1930s. It represents aspects of the Nuremberg Laws, introduced by the Nazis in 1935.

The two main parts of the Nuremberg Laws were the Reich Citizenship Law and the Law for the Protection of German Blood and Honour. The first law removed German citizenship from Jews. The Nazi authorities later clarified that the law also applied to Roma and Black people. The second banned intermarriage between Jews and Aryans, 'Aryan' being a spurious racial category to which the Nazis claimed 'true Germans' belonged.

The Nuremberg Laws codified who was categorised as a Jew, and Nabe's diagram shows an aspect of this. Jews are represented on the diagram with the blue diagonal stripes, and the text reads:

> *Explanation of the Reich Citizenship Law. Whoever is descended from three fully Jewish grandparents is a Jew. Whoever has two fully Jewish grandparents is a mixed Jew* ('Jüdischer Mischling'). *He who is a member of a Jewish religious community or is married to a Jew is a Jew.*

Other parts of Nabe's project commemorate Nazi 'heroes' and describe Hitler's 'achievements'. The document illustrates the way that school students in Nazi Germany were encouraged to learn about Nazi policy and ideology and celebrate Nazism.

Nothing is known about Gerda Nabe other than that she seems to have attended a technical school in Celle, Lower Saxony. Her school project work was discovered in 1946 by a British serviceman stationed in Germany amongst some papers in the office he was assigned to in Celle. The documents were deposited in the Library by the serviceman's family in 1996.

GERMANY and YOU

FEATURES

Cover Picture: Gate Tower in Rothenburg, *by August Rumbucher, Jr.*

Volume VI Number **4**

BERLIN W 9, EICHHORNSTRASSE 10

WIKING VERLAG

Germany and You, 1936

This English-language periodical, published in Germany by Wiking Verlag, promoted positive messages about Nazi Germany in an ostensibly non-ideological way. The publisher had voluntarily cooperated with the process of Nazification (*Gleichschaltung*) of German businesses in 1934. Articles in this particular edition include features highlighting German economic modernity alongside pieces on the German countryside and German culture.

A 'Reader's Comments' insert provides testimonials from individuals, schools and libraries around the world who purportedly subscribed to the journal, including Clifton College, Bristol who are said to have commented:

> *it is indeed a most attractive publication, and I shall give my pupils an opportunity of reading it.*

A subscriber in Chicago is quoted as saying:

> *your magazine comes as a messenger of reality from across the Atlantic, and once here, acts as a bulwark of verity against the onslaughts of the foreign press.*

The front cover of this particular edition has a stamp of the *Deutscher Fichte Bund* (DFB), a German association named after philosopher Johann Gottlieb Fichte. During the Nazi era, the organisation distributed Nazi propaganda abroad and worked under Goebbels' Ministry for Public Enlightenment and Propaganda. DFB's possession of this volume would suggest that they regarded *Germany and You* as part of this effort.

It is not known when copies of *Germany and You* came into The Wiener Library's collections.

„Hier, Kleiner, haſt du etwas ganz Süßes! Aber dafür müßt ihr beide mit mir gehen…"

Ernst Hiemer and Philipp Rupprecht: *Der Giftpilz* (*The Poisonous Mushroom*), 1938

This children's book, published during the Nazi era in Germany, features some of the best-known antisemitic propaganda images targeted at children. The book forms part of the Library's collection of children's books from Nazi Germany. It was donated by German-British filmmaker, curator and artist Lutz Becker, a long-time supporter of the Library.

The Poisonous Mushroom was published by Julius Streicher (1885-1946), a regional leader in Germany during the Nazi era. Streicher was the founder and publisher of the virulently antisemitic pro-Nazi newspaper, *Der Stürmer* ('The Stormer' or 'Stormtrooper').

The book was not an official Nazi Party production, but Streicher had up to 100,000 copies of it published and distributed, particularly to German schools. The book describes how children might identify and protect themselves from Jews. It is one of a number of similar publications produced by Streicher, Ernst Hiemer, a former teacher, and the illustrator 'Fips'.

Julius Streicher was convicted and executed for crimes against humanity in 1946 at the Nuremberg War Crimes trials.

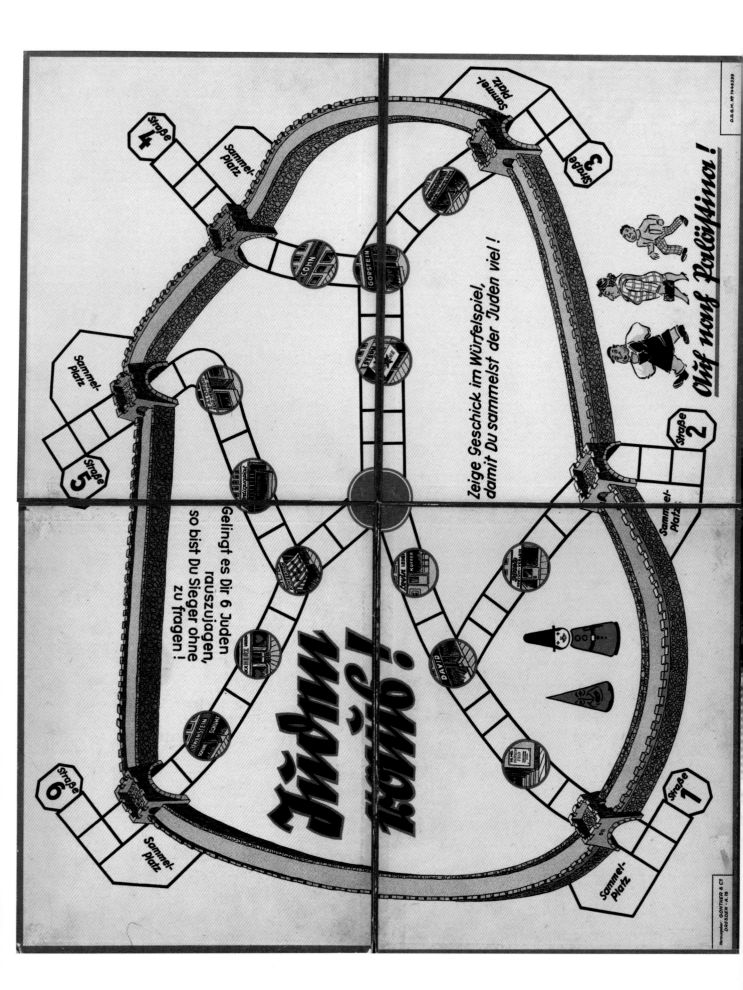

Juden Raus! (Jews Out!) boardgame, 1938

This game was produced privately by Günther and Company in Dresden and distributed by the games company Fabricus. The board features crude antisemitic imagery, and the aim of the game is to expel Jews from the city. Beyond the city walls a slogan reads *Auf nach Palästina!* (Off to Palestine!)

Although the game was not produced or endorsed by the Nazi Party and does not feature any Nazi insignia, its name mirrors a Nazi slogan and its themes reflect antisemitic Nazi policies of forced deportations of Jews and the seizure of Jewish property.

The game was produced in a context of deteriorating conditions for Jews in Germany. The Nazi policy of 'Aryanisation' (seizure) of property intensified during 1938, and many Jewish families lost their homes and businesses, and other items of value.

The Library has three copies of *Juden Raus!* at least one of which has been in the collection since the 1940s.

Der letzte Appell
Von Gustav Regler

„Goebbels wirft den Intellektuellen vor,
sie hätten „keinen Mut", weil sie keine
Lust hatten, im Herbst vorigen Jahres für
die volksfremden Interessen des deutschen
Grosskapitals in den Krieg zu ziehen...
Sie hatten den Mut, wie Goebbels selbst
schreibt, ihm bei den Sammelaktionen vor
dem 1...

Tomate Merveille des Marc...
Tomate Wunder des Marktes
Pomodoro Meraviglia dei Mercati

A tomato seed pack concealing an anti-Nazi pamphlet, c.1939

The pamphlet contained within this packet of tomato seeds was written by the exiled German Communist writer Gustav Regler (1898-1963). In it, Regler denounced the Nazi Party's attacks on intellectuals in the Third Reich. It is part of an extensive and varied collection of anti-Nazi writing held by the Library and known as *Tarnschriften* – 'hidden writing'.

Gustav Regler was a First World War veteran, born in 1898 in Merzig in the German Empire. He served in the International Brigades during the Spanish Civil War, and his books were banned in the Third Reich.

Approximately 1,000 covert and concealed publications were produced by a variety of anti-Nazi groups between 1933 and 1945 as a form of political resistance to Nazi rule. They were created with the intention of inspiring dissent and disseminating information to counter Nazi propaganda in Germany. The Nazi era saw a significant expansion in the production of *Tarnschriften*, but they were a long-established form of political communication and resistance in Germany. During the Second Reich (1871-1917), the SPD published camouflaged clandestine pamphlets to secretly spread their ideas and gain political traction in response to Chancellor Otto von Bismarck's Anti-Socialist Laws of 1878. In the Nazi era, *Tarnschriften* were made covertly, often in neighbouring countries like Czechoslovakia and France, from where they were then smuggled into the Third Reich.

Tarnschriften were produced by many different groups, including the Communist Party of Germany (KPD), Social Democratic Party (SPD), Catholic organisations and the right-wing anti-Nazi group The Black Front. To avoid repercussions, some *Tarnschriften* were published anonymously.

The Library's records show that most of our *Tarnschriften* collection was received in 1959. However, the origin of the collection is not known. It has been suggested that it may have been a collection originally accumulated by the Gestapo.

Dorfjude aus der Inneren Slowakei. Er schützt sein Enkelkind,
das er nicht aus den Armen lassen will, durch die eigene Kör-
perwärme vor dem Frost.

Berthold Birnbach: Jews on the Hungarian-Czech border, November 1938

This photograph is one of a set of images held by The Wiener Holocaust Library depicting some of the Jews who were deported by far-right nationalist Slovak militias and the Hungarian authorities to a newly established Hungarian-Czech border region in 1938. Part of Slovakia had been handed to Hungary by fascist Germany and Italy in the First Vienna Award of 2 November 1938. Czechoslovak authorities refused to allow the group entry. Stranded in a kind of no-man's land between the two countries without proper supplies for a week, the deportees were given aid primarily by local Jewish communities. The photographs in this collection capture the fate of a group of expelled Jewish refugees near Miloslavov.

The photographer is believed to be Berthold Birnbach, born in Vienna in 1903. He is thought to have fled Austria in March 1938 and settled in Prague, Czechoslovakia, where he worked as a journalist. According to a contemporary police report found in the Czech national archives, Birnbach 'collected and compiled picture stories for foreign journals' and travelled around the country. Birnbach probably took this photograph when he accompanied Jewish social workers to the Czechoslovakian-Hungarian borderland in late November 1938. How and when the prints then came to England is uncertain, but it seems to have been part of an effort to raise awareness about the plight of the deportees.

The collection held by The Wiener Holocaust Library comprises fourteen different images and eleven duplicates. Originally, all the prints seem to have been pasted into a paper booklet. Typewritten captions in German pasted next to the pictures provide details on their content and context. The collection also contains a contemporary report in English by Czech Jewish social worker Maria Schmolka (Schmolková) about her visit to Miloslavov and similar refugee camps in the Czechoslovakian-Hungarian borderland.

Verhafteten korrekt behandelt. Dagegen wurden die im Asyl für Obdach-lose Untergebrachten schon dort in der schmählichsten Weise misshan-delt. Ein Vorgesetzter, er wurde als Werkleutnant bezeichnet, der den Befehl über diese Verhafteten hatte, legte es offensichtlich ganz systematisch darauf an, die Leute in der Nacht nicht zur Ruhe kommen zu lassen. Dieser Beamte erschien in ganz kurzen Zeitabständen, don-nerte die Leute an, liess sie aufstehen und in dem Saal einen Hauer-lauf veranstalten, bei dem auch Männer über 60 Jahre über Hindernisse hinwegspringen mussten. Andere, die infolge sichtbaren Leidens daran nicht beteiligt werden konnten, mussten einen Kreis herum bilden und dabei singen: "Weisst du wieviel Sternlein stehen?"

Im Laufe des Vormittags wurden an den einzelnen Stellen die über

Baureste Sorge zu tragen. Die Synagogen und die Friedhofsbaulichkeiten sind vollständig dem Erdboden gleich gemacht worden.

Gleichzeitig mit der Brandstiftung dieser Gemeindebaulichkeiten wurde auch das der Herrenkonfektionsfirma Bamberger & Hertz am Augustus-platz Ecke Grimmaische Strasse gehörige Grundstück in Brand gesteckt. Schon in der Morgenausgabe des 10.November wurde über diesen Brand be-richtet und die Sache so dargestellt, als hätte der Inhaber der Firma das Grundstück selbst in Brand gesteckt, um einen Versicherungsbetrug zu begehen, nachdem die Verkaufschancen für das Unternehmen in der Zeit sehr schlecht geworden und damit auch seine Vermögensverhältnisse sehr beeinträchtigt gewesen seien. Das Grundstück beherbergt nach der Seite des Augustusplatzes in einem Gebäudeteil auch ein Kaffee, das dort das Erdgeschoss und die erste Etage inne hat. Der Brand verlief so, dass die Geschäftsräume der Firma Bamberger & Hertz restlos ausbrannten, jedoch die Räume des Kaffees und auch die darüber liegenden Büroräume vollständig unberührt blieben. Der öffentlich so Verdächtigte stellte sich daraufhin ohne weiteres der Staatsanwaltschaft, die jedoch erklärte, dass gegen ihn nichts vorläge. Daraufhin begab er sich in die Wohnung, wurde verhaftet und ins Konzentrationslager gebracht, und nachdem er dort sieben Wochen festgehalten worden war, erneut ins Polizeigefäng-nis eingeliefert. Dort versuchte man, von ihm ein Protokoll zu erzwin-gen, worin er die Beschuldigung der Brandstiftung in irgendeiner Form anerkannte. Er weigerte sich, auch als man von ihm nur eine Erklärung verlangte, dass der gegen ihn vorliegende Verdacht von ihm nicht rest-los habe aufgeklärt werden können. Schliesslich wurde er auf freien Fuss gesetzt.

Das grosse Geschäftshaus der Firma Uri Gebrüder wurde relativ wenig beschädigt. Es wurden nur die zahlreichen Schaufenster zerstört und die Schaufensterauslagen verschwanden. Später wurden die Warenbe-stände durch einen Treuhänder verwertet und nach Abwicklung das Grund-stück für die Textilmesse neu hergerichtet und verwendet.

In zahlreichen Wohnungen erschienen kleinere und grössere Rotten und zerstörten sinnlos die Einrichtungen. Möbel wurden zertrümmert, und mit besonderem Behagen wurden Spiegel und Kristallsachen und ähnliche Gegenstände zerschmettert.

Am frühen Morgen begannen Verhaftungen. Sie wurden teils ordnungs-mässig durch Beamte der Kriminalpolizei oder der Gestapo meist unter Mitwirkung von S.A. und S.S. Leuten vorgenommen, teils aber auch kamen Rotten von offenbar unbefugten Menschen und holten aus den Wohnungen jüdische Männer heraus, um sie der Polizeibehörde zuzuführen. Im Stadt-teil Eutritzsch wurden auch die Frauen zunächst mitgenommen, sie wurden alle, Männer und Frauen, zum Teil auch mit Kindern auf einem öffentli-chen Platz aufgestellt, sodann wurden die Frauen alle, von den Männern ein kleiner Teil wieder entlassen, die anderen, ohne irgendwelche Gegen-stände mitnehmen zu dürfen, abgeführt. In der Gegend des Zoologischen Gartens jagte man die Verhafteten an die dort fliessende Parthe, nötig-te sie, eine Treppe, die hinunterführt, hinabzusteigen und trieb sie so bis dicht an das Wasser heran, liess sie allerdings zum Teil später wieder in ihre Wohnungen zurück. Den anderen Teil nahmen Polizeibeamte mit, um sie ins Konzentrationslager zu überführen. Die Festgenommenen wurden zunächst zum Teil in das Gerichtsgefängnis, zum Teil in das Asyl für Obdachlose gebracht.

In den beiden Abteilungen des Gerichtsgefängnisses wurden die

haus kamen. Dort wurden nach ... Bade dem Arzt unter der Meldung vorge-führt : " Schutzhaftjude N.N. meldet sich gehorsamst zur Stelle " Ich wie die meisten Häftlinge bekamen im Beisein des Stabsarztes Ohr-feigen rechts und links,weil die Meldung nicht laut genug war. Untersuchung wurde nicht vorgenommen; es wurde nur gefragt : "krank

Eyewitness accounts of *Kristallnacht,* c.1939

This eyewitness account of some of the events of *Kristallnacht,* the attack on the Jewish communities of Germany and Austria on 9-10 November 1938, is one of over 350 such reports collected by The Wiener Holocaust Library's predecessor organisation, the JCIO, in Amsterdam in the immediate days and weeks following *Kristallnacht.*

Kristallnacht (sometimes known as The Night of Broken Glass or The November Pogrom) saw the Nazi Party leadership orchestrate a wave of attacks on Jews across the Third Reich. Synagogues were burnt, shops smashed and Jewish homes ransacked. Hundreds of Jews were murdered and thousands assaulted. Many women were sexually assaulted. Around 30,000 Jewish men were arrested and sent to concentration camps. Conditions in the camps were brutal.

Through its network of contacts in Germany, Austria and the Netherlands, the JCIO received reports of the horrific attack almost as soon as it began. The first report is dated 9 November 1938, and they come from right across the German Reich. These reports were mainly received in November and December 1938, and they were typed up and collated in the form seen here in early 1939. The reports seem to have come to the JCIO by phone, by letter and through intermediaries. Some of the reporters were Jews who fled the country during or after *Kristallnacht*; others were still based in the country.

This particular report is from Leipzig. It describes synagogue burnings, attacks on Jewish cemeteries, businesses, homes and community leaders, and the arrest of Jewish men. The perpetrators are identified by the author as members of the SA and SS and also 'mobs'.

Using the evidence that they gathered, the JCIO produced reports of *Kristallnacht* that were distributed globally to Jewish organisations, journalists and others.

W. Bosholm
vorm. Weingarten

Ludwig Neuman, c.1915 and late December 1938

At the time of *Kristallnacht* Ludwig Neumann (1896-1970) became one of approximately 30,000 Jewish men arrested and sent to a concentration camp; in his case Dachau near Munich. During the First World War, he had served in the German army for which he was awarded an Iron Cross.

Neumann was the owner and manager of his family's firm, Neumann and Mendel, a large clothing manufacturing business that had been founded in 1889. In the month before *Kristallnacht*, Neumann was forced by the Nazis to surrender the firm to Joseph Herbring, a Nazi supporter: this seizure of property was part of the Nazi policy of 'Aryanisation'.

The later photograph seems to have been taken by a family member on Ludwig Neumann's release from Dachau, in late December 1938. Documents in the Wiener Library's collections reveal that conditions in the camp were particularly poor and the image indicates that Neumann had been mistreated.

Ludwig Neumann was released by the Nazi authorities on the condition that he emigrated, and Neumann, a keen photographer, produced multiple copies of this image: he may have used it to support applications for visas.

Ultimately, Neumann, his sister Luise and mother Dina were able to obtain visas to come to Britain before the outbreak of the Second World War. The family firm exported to Britain and so it is possible that British business connections enabled them to find the sponsorship that their visas would have likely required.

Despite being a Jewish refugee from Nazism, Neumann was interned by the British as a so-called 'enemy alien' in 1940. He later served in the Home Guard as an anti-aircraft gunner.

Ludwig Neumann died in 1970. His cousins eventually deposited his extensive business and personal papers and photographs with The Wiener Holocaust Library.

Soup kitchen of the Jewish Community March 1938-February 1939.

III	IV	V	VI	VII	VIII	IX	X	XI	XII	I	II

1000

Report of the Jewish Community of Vienna, January-February 1939

This report records the rising impoverishment experienced by the Jews in pre-war Vienna. It is part of a collection of material relating to the Jewish Community of Vienna held by The Wiener Holocaust Library. The graph shows the huge and very rapid rise in the use of the Jewish Community of Vienna's soup kitchen in early 1939.

Austria had been annexed by Germany in March 1938, an event that triggered an explosion of antisemitic violence in the country. In Vienna, Jews were subjected to violent attacks, abuse and humiliations such as being forced to clean pro-Austrian slogans from the streets with caustic soda. Shops and homes were looted. Nazi antisemitic laws were subsequently introduced, and Jewish property subject to 'Aryanisation': that is, their forced handover to pro-Nazi Germans and Austrians. Jews were also frequently forced out of their jobs. The consequences of persecution and rising impoverishment for Vienna's Jewish community can be seen starkly in this graph.

Around 130,000 Jews fled Austria at this time, and 66,000 Austrian Jews were ultimately murdered during the Holocaust.

By the time that this report was produced, the Jewish Community of Vienna had been compelled by the Nazis to change its name from *Israelitische Kultusgemeinde Wien* to *Jüdische Gemeinde Wien* and forced to work in assisting in the process of Jewish forced migration and later deportation from Austria.

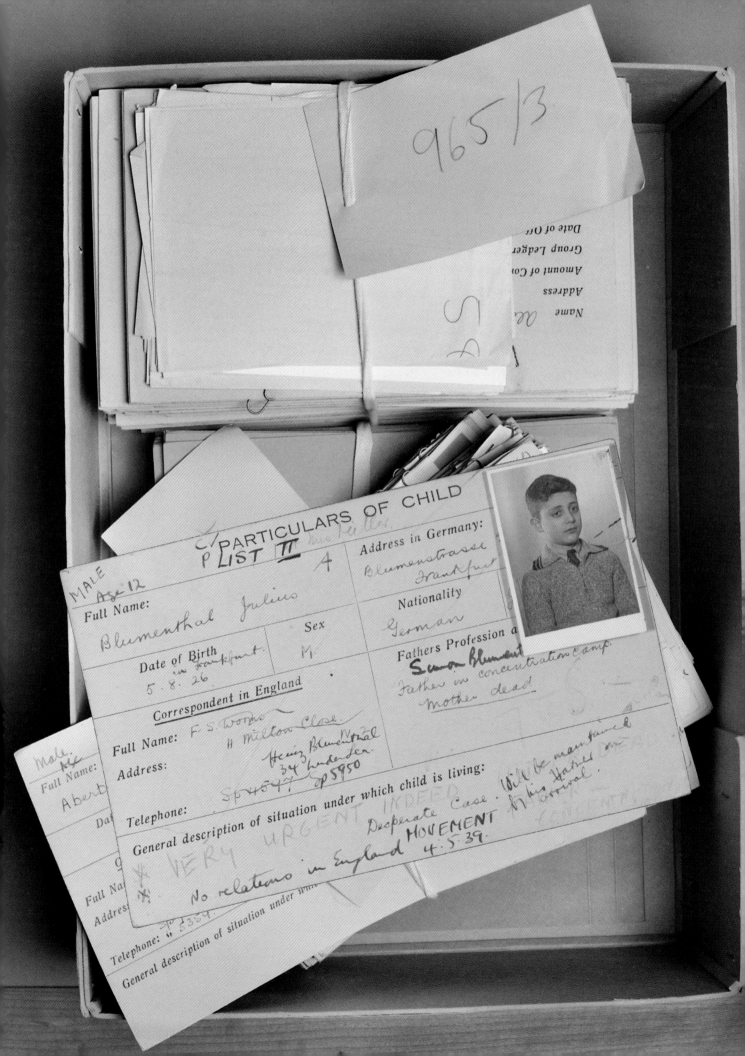

965/3

Name
Address
Amount of Co
Group Ledger
Date of O
Date of Off

C/ PARTICULARS OF CHILD
P LIST II

Address in Germany:
Blumenstrasse
Frankfurt

MALE
Age 12
Full Name:
Blumenthal Julius
in Frankfurt.

Nationality
German

Date of Birth
5. 8. 26

Sex
M

Fathers Profession a
Simon Blument
Father in concentration camp.
mother dead.

Correspondent in England

Full Name: F. S. Woods
H Millow Close.

Heinz Blumenthal
34 Lindender
SP 4547 ØP 5950

Address:

Telephone:

General description of situation under which child is living:
Desperate Case. Will be maintained
by his father on
arrival.

VERY URGENT INDEED.
No relations in England. MOVEMENT
4. 5. 39.

Male
Full Name:
Abert

Da

Full Na
Address

Telephone: ℉ 5359
General description of situation under whic

Record card from the Hampstead Garden Suburb Care Committee collection, c.1939

This record card gives details of a twelve-year-old boy, Julius Blumenthal from Frankfurt, who sought refuge in Britain. It is part of the institutional records of a small charitable organisation set up to try to help children who sought to come to Britain on the *Kindertransport* scheme.

The *Kindertransport* was the rescue of around 10,000 mainly Jewish children, predominantly from Germany and Austria, between late 1938 and early 1940. The scheme was a visa-waiver programme, and it simplified the process of bringing child refugees to Britain. The British government permitted the *Kindertransport* in the aftermath of the events of *Kristallnacht* in November 1938, but did not organise or fund it. Various Jewish community and voluntary sector organisations managed the programme, including arranging lists of children, transport and sponsorship to enable the children to come (each child was supposed to be sponsored £50 by someone in Britain), as well as providing placements and welfare checks for children after they arrived in the UK.

Julius Blumenthal's card is revealing: it states that his mother was dead and his father in a concentration camp. His case is described as 'very urgent' and 'desperate'. There is an address in London for his brother Heinz recorded on the card. Heinz was a *Kindertransportee* and his record card is also held in this collection.

Julius Blumenthal's card records 'Movement: 4.5.39', which may indicate that the case was passed to the Refugee Children's Movement, a group that coordinated much of the *Kindertransport*.

We do not know the fate of Julius Blumenthal and his father. Recent research indicates that the majority of children on the *Kindertransport* lost one or both of their parents in the Holocaust.

The TOLERANCE AND SYMPATHY of Britain and the British Commonwealth

THE traditional tolerance and sympathy of Britain and the British Commonwealth towards the Jews is something which every British Jew appreciates profoundly. On his part he does all in his power to express his loyalty to Britain and the British Commonwealth, in word and in deed, by personal service and by communal effort.

This loyalty comes first and foremost, and every Refugee should realise how deeply it is felt.

The Jewish Community in Britain will do its very utmost to welcome and maintain all Refugees, to educate their Children, to care for the Aged and the Sick—and to assist in every possible way in creating new homes for them overseas. A great many Christians, in all walks of life, have spontaneously associated themselves with this work. All that we ask you in return is to carry out to your utmost the following lines of conduct. Regard them, please, as **duties to which you are in honour bound :**

Die Toleranz und Sympathie von Gross-Britannien und des Britischen Staatenbundes

Gross-Britanniens und des Britischen Staatenbundes althergebrachte Toleranz und Sympathie den Juden gegenüber ist etwas, was jeder britische Jude zutiefst würdigt. In Wort und Tat, durch persönliche Dienste und gemeinsame Anstrengungen tut er seinerseits alles, was in seiner Macht steht, um seiner Loyalität zu Gross-Britannien und dem Britischen Staatenbund Ausdruck zu verleihen.

Diese Loyalität kommt zu allererst, und jeder Flüchtling sollte einsehen, wie tief empfunden sie wird.

Die Jüdische Gemeinde in Gross-Britannien wird ihr Äusserstes tun, um alle Flüchtlinge aufzunehmen und zu unterhalten, ihre Kinder zu erziehen, für die Alten und Kranken zu sorgen—und ihnen in jeder möglichen Weise behilflich zu sein, neue Heimstätten in überseeischen Ländern zu schaffen. Eine grosse Anzahl von Christen aus allen Schichten der Bevölkerung hat sich mit uns zu dieser Aufgabe verbunden. Alles, was wir von Ihnen dafür verlangen, ist, sich in Ihrem Benehmen genauestens nach den folgenden Regeln zu richten.

German Jewish Aid Committee and the Board of Deputies of British Jews: *While You Are In England: Helpful Information and Guidance for Every Refugee, c.1939*

In 1938, as the number of Jewish refugees arriving in Britain increased, the German Jewish Aid Committee, founded in 1933 and also known as the Jewish Refugee Committee (JRC), stepped up its efforts to assist those arriving. This pamphlet was produced by the Committee and the Board of Deputies to help refugees integrate into British life.

The content reflects the concerns that some in the Anglo-Jewish community had about the new Jewish refugees. It advises refugees to 'refrain from speaking German in the streets' and not to 'make yourself conspicuous by speaking loudly' nor to 'criticise any Government regulations'.

This pamphlet is one of The Wiener Holocaust Library's extensive collection of pamphlets from the 1930s and 1940s, most of which were published in Britain. Pamphlets were a common mode of public communication during this era and an essential part of political campaigning and of public information campaigns. The Wiener Holocaust Library has been collecting pamphlets from the Nazi era for many decades.

Ehefrau

Lichtbild

Unterschrift des Paßinhabers

Charlotte Pilpel

~~und seiner Ehefrau~~

Es wird hiermit bescheinigt, daß der Inhaber die durch
das obenstehende Lichtbild dargestellte Person ist und
die darunter befindliche Unterschrift eigenhändig voll-
zogen hat.

Wien , den 15. FEB. 1939

Wagner

2

PERSONENBESCHREIBUNG

		Ehefrau
Beruf	*Mittelschülerin*	
Geburtsort	*Wien*	
Geburtstag	*16. III. 1921*	
Wohnort	*Wien*	
Gestalt	*mittel*	
Gesicht	*oval*	
Farbe der Augen	*braun*	
Farbe des Haares	*d. braun*	
Besond. Kennzeichen	*—*	

KINDER

Name	Alter	Geschlecht

3

Charlotte Pilpel: travel document with stamps, c.1939

This travel document, a form of passport belonging to Charlotte (Lotte) Pilpel (b.1921), forms part of one of The Wiener Holocaust Library's many collections of documents relating to the experiences of Jewish individuals and families who came as refugees to Britain during the 1930s and occasionally as Holocaust survivors after the war. Many of these kinds of documents have been deposited with the Library in recent decades.

Charlotte Pilpel was born to a Jewish family in Vienna, the daughter of Emil and Serla Pilpel. Lotte had an elder sister, Fanny, born in 1916. After the annexation of Austria by Nazi Germany, life became increasingly difficult for the Pilpel family. In May 1939, Lotte Pilpel received permission to emigrate to Britain, where a shortage of servants enabled migrants to settle using a domestic service visa. Many Jewish women from Vienna came to Britain this way.

In order to emigrate, Pilpel had to be declared medically fit by the British authorities and Nazi Germany did not make it easy for Jewish refugees to leave: émigrés had to pay a 'flight' tax and acquire exit and entry visas. Pilpel's Third Reich Jewish passport contains stamps relating to all of these requirements, as well as her visa to the United Kingdom 'for domestic employment'. Pilpel's sister followed her to Britain on the same scheme.

Pilpel's parents remained in Vienna following their daughters' departure, and continued to try to acquire visas to emigrate to the United Kingdom. They were ultimately unsuccessful, and on 20 May 1942 they were deported to Minsk. Six days later they were murdered by an SS killing squad.

199

SUNDAY 14th

MONDAY 15th

TUESDAY 16th

WEDNESDAY 17th

THURSDAY 18TH

Have been informed transport is going to Australia. Scheduled to take six weeks. Many nervous breakdowns, terrible scenes. Hunger strike

FRIDAY 19TH

Have drafted telegram to Mr. Churchill asking for change of route. Protest handed to Commander.

SATURDAY 20TH

Many suitcases have been opened by soldiers bayonets. Contents taken out. Valuables kept by soldiers.

MEMO.

Jewish Torah saved from Munich Synagogue thrown into the sea by soldiers.

Herbert Malinow: diary, 1940

Herbert Malinow (b.1920) was a Jew from Breslau in Germany (now Wroclaw, Poland). He came to Britain in 1936 to escape Nazi persecution and was followed by his parents in 1939. Malinow was interned as an 'enemy alien' in June 1940, during a period when the British authorities sought to hold captive all German, Austrian and Italian men living in Britain and aged between 16 and 65, as well as some women. Many of those arrested and interned in this period were refugees from Nazism and fascism.

Malinow was amongst a group of around 2,000 internees, four-fifths of whom were Jewish, sent to Australia aboard the notorious HMT *Dunera* by the British authorities. The ship was very overcrowded and conditions were poor. Furthermore, the crew looted the possessions of the internees, as Malinow recorded in this diary that he kept on the ship. On 15 July 1940, he wrote: 'everyone has been bodily searched. False teeth taken away. Wedding rings forced off fingers'.

Malinow was held in Hay internment camp in New South Wales, Australia until his return to Britain in August 1941. Thereafter he joined the Pioneer Corps of the British Army.

This diary is one of two written by an internee on the Dunera held by The Wiener Holocaust Library. The other one is that of Bernard Simon (see page 23).

No. 38

May 18th 1941   Price 2d

the Onchan Pioneer

POINTS OF VIEW

expected arriva...
pervaded the Ca...
night. Almost e...
new rumour as o...
Camp between or...
periods, until ...
here, among th...
Nazi-Hell from ...
there had occu...
in Germany an...
out. But some...
gem of the Na...
smuggled into ...

people are...
still have...

+).(Vorsi...
Cante...

..., and the...
...d fire through the...

A DEVIL FLIES OUT OF HIS OWN CREATED HELL

The *Onchan Pioneer*, the journal created by internees of the Onchan camp, May 1941

Onchan was one of a number of camps for internees on the Isle of Man: the British authorities generally located the camps away from major centres of population. From July 1940, the Onchan internees started to produce a camp newspaper, *The Onchan Pioneer*. Articles and features in the *Pioneer* reflected the intellectual and artistic interests and talents of some of the inmates: Onchan held a particularly high number of academics and artists and the camp often held art exhibitions, lectures and classes. The *Pioneer* also contained articles expressing the desire of many internees to assist Britain in the war effort. Many internees later joined the Pioneer Corps of the British Army.

Around 1,300 German and Austrian internees were held in Onchan between June 1940 and July 1941, by which time most Jewish internees had been released. Later it was used to house Italian internees. The camp finally closed in November 1944.

The Wiener Holocaust Library has a complete set of editions of *The Onchan Pioneer*.

Audience at a children's play in the Łódź ghetto, *c.*1940-43

The Łódź ghetto in German-occupied Poland was the second largest ghetto in Occupied Europe, after Warsaw. Established in 1940, 210,000 Jews were held there. The ghetto became a large industrial centre and it was only finally liquidated in 1944. Tight control of the ghetto by the *Judenrat* (Jewish Council) in Łódź made armed resistance difficult. There was considerable political, spiritual and cultural resistance in Łódź, efforts to sustain religious and cultural life that, in the face of Nazi dehumanisation of Jews and policies of mass murder, could be considered to be a form of resistance to Nazism.

This photograph of a musical recital appears to reflect the cultural life of the ghetto. Its origins are uncertain: we do not know who took the photograph or how it came to be in our collections. Yad Vashem has a copy (and other photographs) of the same event which they describe as a children's play. However, in our collection it is described as 'a musical evening in Łódź ghetto'. The Wiener Holocaust Library's photographic archive contains a number of images accessioned many years ago, the origins of which remain obscure.

The head of the *Judenrat*, Chaim Rumkowski (1877-1944), is pictured in the front row, second from the right. Rumkowski had hoped that his cooperation with the Nazi authorities, and the repressive regime that he established, would save the inhabitants of the ghetto. He was widely resented and likely killed by other prisoners on his arrival in Auschwitz.

German soldiers filming the Pogrom of Lvov, 1941

This photograph shows German Army (*Wehrmacht*) soldiers in a propaganda unit film a massacre of Jews carried out by the Ukrainian National Militia as part of the Lvov pogroms of June-July 1941. Other pogroms in Lvov at this time were perpetrated by *Einsatzgruppe C*. The image was probably taken on 30 June 1941, the day the Germans occupied the city and the pogroms began.

Lvov was occupied by the Soviet Union in September 1939, and then by Germany from June 1941. During the pogroms, Jews were forced to carry out acts of public humiliation such as cleaning the street with their bare hands, and they were beaten and stripped. Approximately 6,000 Jews died in the violence.

This photograph was taken by a member of the *Wehrmacht*. It shows his comrades photographing the pogrom. A crowd watches the attacks and a woman standing in the background seems to be smiling. The image raises questions about the nature of local collaboration and the role of bystanders to atrocities.

The photograph was one of a series sent to The Wiener Holocaust Library in the 1990s. Most of the photographs in the collection show images of attacks on the Jews of Lvov, including sexualised attacks on women and girls. The photographs were said to have been found in an attic: the identity of the photographer was not revealed. Other archives also have copies of some images from this series, but the Wiener Library's set appears to be the most extensive.

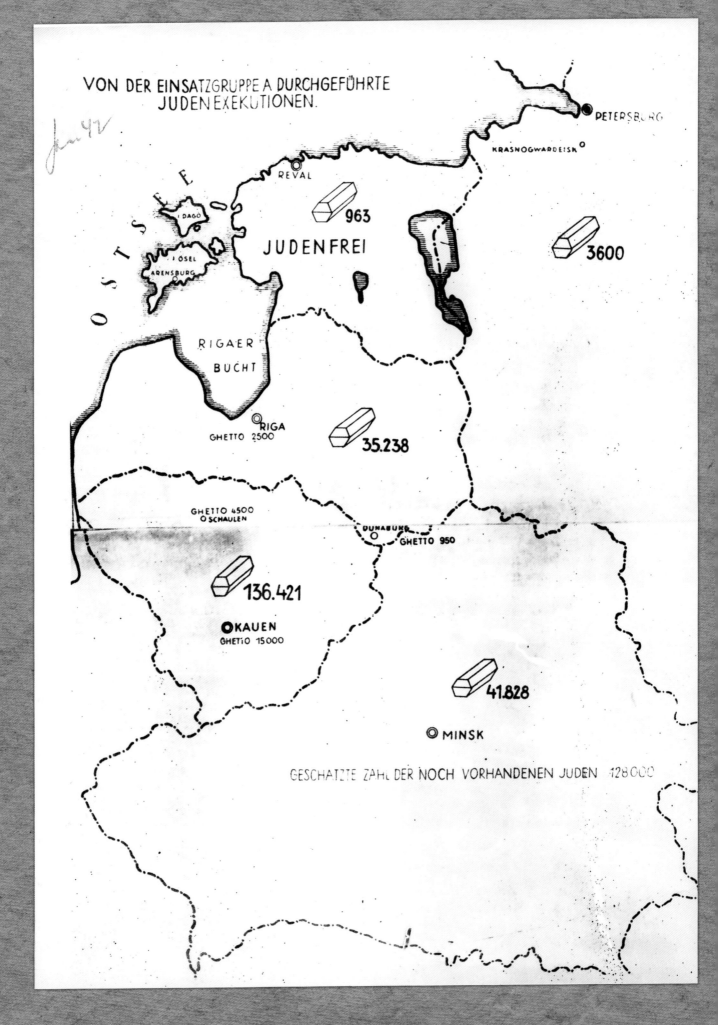

VON DER EINSATZGRUPPE A DURCHGEFÜHRTE
JUDENEXEKUTIONEN.

Jan 42

PETERSBURG

KRASNOGWARDEISK

O
S
T
S
E
E

I DAGO

REVAL

963

JUDENFREI

3600

I ÖSEL
ARENSBURG

RIGAER

BUCHT

RIGA
GHETTO 2500

35.238

GHETTO 4500
O SCHAULEN

DUNABURG
GHETTO 950

136.421

O KAUEN
GHETTO 15000

41.828

O MINSK

GESCHÄTZTE ZAHL DER NOCH VORHANDENEN JUDEN 128000

The Stahlecker Report: 'Jewish Executions Carried Out by *Einsatzgruppe A*', 15 October 1941

This map was part of the Stahlecker Report, produced by SS Commander Walter Stahlecker (1900-1942) as part of a secret report detailing the mass murder of Jews carried out by the group that Stahlecker commanded, *Einsatzgruppe A*. The *Einsatzgruppen* (Task Forces) were SS death squads which followed the German Army after their invasion of the Soviet Union in June 1941, orchestrating and committing mass murders of the Nazis' 'racial' and ideological enemies: Jews, Roma, and Communists. *Einsatzgruppen* carried out mass shootings and mass arrests. Some of the murders that occurred in Soviet territories were perpetrated not by the SS but by local collaborators and local militia groups, such as occurred in Lithuania and Ukraine.

The map indicates the number of Jews murdered by *Einsatzgruppe A* in Russia, Estonia, Latvia, Lithuania and Belarus: numbers are recorded beside coffins for each territory. At the bottom of the map, it records that an estimate of 128,000 Jews remained alive in these areas.

British and American prosecutors at the Nuremberg War Crimes Trials entered this document in evidence. The Wiener Library assisted the War Crimes Trials in their work and in return was given a substantial quantity of these documents.

REPUBLIC OF POLAND

Ministry of Foreign Affairs

THE MASS EXTERMINATION of JEWS in GERMAN OCCUPIED POLAND

NOTE

addressed to the Governments of the
United Nations on December 10th, 1942,
and other documents

*Published on behalf of the Polish
Ministry of Foreign Affairs by*

HUTCHINSON & CO. (Publishers) LTD.
LONDON : NEW YORK : MELBOURNE
Price: Threepence Net.

The Polish Government in Exile: *The Mass Extermination of Jews in German-occupied Poland*, c.1943

It is a common misconception that there was little or no information available in Britain about the mass murder of Jews until the liberation of Bergen-Belsen camp by the British Army on 15 April 1945. However, there were a number of newspaper and other reports describing the Nazi attempts to annihilate the Jews of Europe circulating long before this. This is one such document, a pamphlet compiled by the Polish government-in-exile.

The pamphlet made public the contents of a note of 10 December 1942 addressed by the Polish government-in-exile to the United Nations detailing the mass extermination of Jews in the Polish territories occupied by Germany. It had been produced at the urging of Jewish Polish underground groups, who collected and supplied much of the information.

Shortly afterwards, the British and US governments issued a joint Allied declaration, describing the Nazi persecution of Jews in Europe. The British Foreign Secretary, Anthony Eden MP, read the declaration in the House of Commons and in the following days it was widely reported in the press.

In March 1943, in response to the Nazi campaign of persecution and murder of the Jews of Europe, the Allies convened a conference in Bermuda. It failed to come up with any meaningful proposals to assist Jewish refugees.

"Four Jews and one Jewess were sentenced to death by a Special Court at Czestochowa for leaving the Ghetto without special permission". "The Governor of Radom has issued orders whereby Jews living in parishes of the district will receive special quarters. If they leave these Jewish quarters without permission, they are liable to the death sentence". (GONIEC KRAKOWSKI, Cracow, 18/12 and 20/12/1941)

15. Oswiecim Concentration Camp "At least 10 per cent. of the 15,000 prisoners, the majority of them Jews, in the concentration camps of Oswiecim are dying each month, according to the report of an escaped prisoner which has reached Polish circles in London. The majority of them die from hunger, exhaustion and the effects of flogging, which is inflicted daily, sometimes on individuals and sometimes on groups. There are also a large number of suicides, which are carried out sometimes by hanging and sometimes by deliberately touching the live wire with which the camp is surrounded. A special crematorium has had to be erected because of the impossibility of burying the huge numbers of dead. Jews and priests are confined in special penal sections of the camp, which is housed in an old artillery barracks, surrounded by three fences of electrified barbed wire. The exterior of the camp is guarded by strong contingents of S.S. men, while the warders inside the camp are recruited from German criminals with the worst records". (JEWISH TELEGRAPHIC AGENCY BULLETIN, 9/1/1942)

c) R u m a n i a

16. Lies - and the Fear of Truth "It will be the business of the Union of Rumanian Jews recently established by Marshal Antonescu, work out, pending the wider European solution of the Jewish problem, a comprehensive survey of Rumanian Jewry with a view to putting them to productive labour that will benefit the whole of the national community. .. Exact statistics of the Jewish share in the various trades will make it possible to destroy the lie, so craftily conceived and cunningly maintained, that important branches of Rumanian industry were exclusively in Jewish hands. It is not at all true that without the Jewish financiers, merchants, and traders, Rumania was doomed to collapse, as has been alleged time and again by malicious agents. Except in the Bukovina .. the Rumanian stake is throughout so strong, and at least capable of being in a very short time strengthened to such an extent, that economic life does not by any means depend for its working on Jewish cooperation. ..

"As for Jewish emigration which had long been considered the perfect solution, it is now thought that, both from the Rumanian and the common European point of view, it would be better if Jewish families did not leave Europe. Experience has shown that, as soon as they had settled abroad, they supplied the common enemy with political propagandists". (DER NEUE TAG, Prague, 3/1/1942; Interview with the "Rumanian Government Commissioner for the Jewish Question", Radu Lecca, "a disciple of Alfred Rosenberg")

d) S l o v a k i a

17. Government by Robbery "The Government Land Office announces that the total amount of Jewish land property transferred to Government ownership, now is 90.771 hectares (roughly 226.930 acres). These included 44.771 hectares of ploughed land, 37.640 hectares of forests, and the rest meadows and pastures, etc. Out of this total amount, Slovak farmers have so far received more than 22.500 acres. The rest is for the time being left in the charge of the former owners". (NEUES WIENER TAGBLATT, Vienna, 3/1/1941)

Jewish News: A bulletin issued periodically by the Jewish Central Information Office

■ DIRECTOR'S CHOICE: TOBY SIMPSON · DIRECTOR OF THE WIENER HOLOCAUST LIBRARY

Between 1939 and 1945, from its base in London, the JCIO distributed information gathered by its employees concerning the war. Increasingly, their work documented escalating persecution and genocide directed against Jews. The *Jewish News* is the second of two bulletins created specifically for the purpose of summarising diverse information on this topic into a digestible format for circulation. The first bulletin, the *Nazis at War*, was started at the suggestion of the British government's Ministry of Information and published fortnightly. It was sent out free of charge to supporters of the JCIO. Dozens of copies were distributed internally among relevant government departments.

From January 1942, *Jewish News* was started with the specific aim of reaching the public with information about the Nazi persecution of Jews. This initiative was instigated by historian and journalist Caesar Aronsfeld, who had joined the Library in 1938.

Jewish News drew attention to mass murder at Auschwitz on several occasions, most strikingly via the report of an escaped prisoner relayed first to the Jewish Telegraphic Agency, and then onwards to recipients of the second bulletin issued on 29 January 1942, a little more than a week after the Wannsee conference had taken place outside Berlin.

The primary audience for this bulletin was the Jewish public, but the publication also aimed to engage non-Jews with the plight of Europe's Jews. This is notable, for example, in the context of the deportation of Hungarian Jews in the summer of 1944, where an article from the *Basler Nachrichten* was cited prominently stating that

> *According to a reliable report, more than 400,000 Hungarian Jews have been deported under inhuman conditions. Those who did not perish on route have been taken to a camp at Oswiecim [Auschwitz], where for two years many hundreds of thousands of Jews have been systematically murdered [...] we appeal to our Christian Hungarian brothers to raise their voices in protest and do all that is possible to end this horrible crime.*

The *Jewish News* bulletins encapsulate the immediacy that sets The Wiener Holocaust Library's collections apart from other archives. Few other documents attest so lucidly to the catastrophe of the Holocaust and humanity's failure to stop it.

WC11962 / WL15724
1574/2/10

Deutsches Rotes Kreuz

Präsidium / Auslandsdienst

Berlin SW 61, Blücherplatz 2

1 FEB. 1943   465538

ANTRAG

an die *Agence Centrale des Prisonniers de Guerre, Genf*
— Internationales Komitee vom Roten Kreuz —
auf Nachrichtenvermittlung

REQUÊTE

de la *Croix-Rouge Allemande, Présidence, Service Etranger*
à l'Agence Centrale des Prisonniers de Guerre, Genève
— Comité International de la Croix-Rouge —
concernant la correspondance

1. **Absender** ..Franz .Israel .Kuhn., Berlin Halensee 1 ..
   Expéditeur   .. .. .. Hektorstr. 20 .. ..

bittet, an
prie de bien vouloir faire parvenir à

Verwandtschaftsgrad: .. Vater .des .Garantiekindes .. ..
schreibt an die Garanten

2. **Empfänger** Millie Levy, Westminster Bank .. ..
   Destinataire London W. 1 , 133 Baker Street
   .. ..

   .. ..

folgendes zu übermitteln / *ce qui suit:*

(Höchstzahl 25 Worte!)
(25 mots au plus!)

Sorry bad news. Mummy emigrated 14th
12.42 by 25.transport. Please appease
Hannele, am terrified myself, but
hoping confidently reunion with family
after the war.

(Datum / *date*)   (Unterschrift / *Signature*)

3. **Empfänger antwortet umseitig**   *Franz Israel Kuhn*
   Destinataire répond au verso

Franz Kuhn: Red Cross telegram, 1942

Red Cross messages are often found in the Library's collections of papers relating to the lives of Jewish refugees from Nazism They are sometimes amongst the final signs of life of those murdered in the Holocaust.

Hannah Kuhn came to Britain on the *Kindertransport* in 1939 aged ten. Her parents were not able to leave Germany. The Kuhn family kept in touch via Red Cross messages and letters sent via an intermediary.

This message is addressed to Millie Levy, one of two sisters who fostered Hannah (referred to here by her father as Hannele) in London, and it was sent care of her bank. In it, Franz Kuhn explained that 'mummy,' by which he meant his wife, Hannah's mother Hertha, had 'emigrated' on 14 December 1942 on transport number 25. She had been arrested and deported east.

Hertha Kuhn was murdered in Auschwitz. Franz Kuhn was deported to Auschwitz on transport number 29 in February 1943, where he was also killed.

Red Cross messages had to be short (no more than 25 words), and could be censored by the German and British authorities. They were supposed to discuss only innocuous subjects. Other messages sent by Franz Kuhn around this time and contained in the Library's document collection have been redacted, but this is a rare example of evidence getting out of Germany in the midst of the Holocaust via an uncensored Red Cross message.

Kuhn presumably sent this message to Millie Levy's bank as he did not want his daughter to find it, but at some point later it was passed by the Levy sisters to Hannah, known as Ann Kirk since her marriage to Bob, another *Kindertransportee*, in 1950. She donated the Red Cross message and other letters to The Wiener Holocaust Library in 1999. In recent decades, Ann and Bob Kirk have worked in Holocaust education.

Der schildwache geht hin
und her.
The sentry goes up & down.
Der Barbier ist aus dem
amerik amerikanischen Lager
... er hat mir die
... schitten. haare
... has come from
... an Camp & cut my
... is haare.
... mir Tabak geben
... umtauchen
... exchange tobacco
... chocolate
... dwache steht
... uns on
... & watches on
... spazirt hin
... ("walks)
... laughing
... war

43
29. Very hot rope soling resumed
6 a parcel for tinned beans and
oddments of clothing still ...
I coming out am completely fed up
... slept last night I will make
... suffer I hope for all this
7 Very hot said ... again
satisfaction but just to wait then
... came today a ... seine
... a whole crowd came on
... Sister Anne, ... Timan
... Garland, Saunders & the
... were called the upshot ...
3 days imprisonment for each
consecutively nice place it's about
... birthday I sat in the
background and took in the whole
scene I pretended to be winding
... after that I played my 3 ...

Esther Pauline Lloyd: diary, c.1943

Esther Pauline Lloyd, née Silver (1906-unknown), moved to Jersey in 1939, where she married. In 1940, following the German occupation of the Channel Islands, Lloyd registered with the authorities as a Jew in accordance with the first Order against the Jews. In Jersey and Guernsey, nine antisemitic regulations (Orders) were introduced between October 1940 and August 1942, encompassing the compulsory registration of those 'deemed to be Jews', the forced sale of Jewish businesses, and a ban on Jews visiting places of public entertainment. Jews in the Channel Islands were also subject to a curfew.

Lloyd was deported in February 1943 to internment camps in France and Germany, along with some of the other British Jews living in the Channel Islands. She kept a diary of her experiences. On 6 May 1943 she wrote, referring to her registration as a Jew in Guernsey, 'never shall I be honest again – if I had not declared myself this wouldn't have happened – it's dreadful'. The diaries also show Lloyd's gradually increasing interest in her Jewish faith. These entries would have posed a considerable risk if they had been discovered by the German authorities.

The Wiener Holocaust Library holds two diaries kept by Lloyd in internment. They cover the period 7 April to 23 November 1943. In addition to a daily account of life in camps at Compiègne and Biberach, the diaries contain notes, addresses, recipes and draft letters.

Lloyd launched an extraordinary campaign against her deportation, writing many letters of complaint protesting her treatment. Her husband lodged an appeal with the Military Command in Jersey for his wife's release.

Remarkably, Esther Pauline Lloyd was repatriated by the German authorities to Jersey on 24 April 1944, probably because she was British.

3.8.43.

Mein geliebtes Kind,

morgen bist Du 16 Jahre alt, bist kein Kind mehr sondern ein junges Mädchen, ein sehr junges Mädchen. [illegible]

In normalen Zeiten hätten wir diesen [illegible] mit allen Gaben u. Blumen gefeiert. Mit vielen schönen u. nützlichen und auch überflüssigen Geschenken, mit gutem Essen u. Trinken, mit Kuchen, Früchten, Eis u. Chokolade. Und vor allem zusammen mit allen Lieben und vielen Freunden und Freundinnen.

Dass dies alles nicht sein kann, erfüllt mich mit grossem Bedauern, aber Du weisst, es geht eigentlich allen Menschen jetzt so, und wir müssen hoffen, dass wir dies alles einmal nachholen können.

Mein eigener 17. Geburtstag war [illegible] harmonisch, und so hätte ich [illegible]

Und ich verspreche Dir, alles was in meinen Kräften steht, will ich daran setzen [illegible]

Mirjam für alle [illegible]

Margarete Wiener: letter to Ruth Wiener, 1943

In this letter, written in Westerbork transit camp, Margarete Wiener (1895-1945), wife of the founder of The Wiener Library, praises her oldest daughter Ruth for her support since the time of their arrest by the Nazis:

> *the moment that you got out of your nice warm bed on that dreadful 20th of July in the early morning* [you have] *helped me so efficiently and sympathetically.*

Wiener and her three daughters spent seven months in Westerbork, from June 1943 to January 1944.

Born in 1895 in Hamburg, Dr Margarete Wiener was an economist. She was also involved in anti-Nazi work from the 1920s onwards in Germany and in Amsterdam at the JCIO in the 1930s, and wrote critiques of Nazi economic policy.

Following the escalation of attacks against the Jewish communities of Germany and Austria at the time of *Kristallnacht* in November 1938, and with the rise of the Nazi Party in Holland, Alfred Wiener felt that he could not count on Amsterdam to be a safe place for his work and his family for much longer. He succeeded in gaining permission for the institution to move to Britain in summer 1939, and obtained visas for some of the JCIO's staff. Margarete Wiener and her daughters received visas in 1940, but had not used them by the time of the German invasion in Holland in May 1940, and as borders closed, they became trapped in Amsterdam.

On 20 June 1943, Margarete, Ruth, Eva and Mirjam were sent to Westerbork transit camp, and then to Bergen-Belsen in January 1944. After a year in the camp, in January 1945, the family were chosen for a rare opportunity to be part of a prisoner exchange scheme between Germany and the United States and were placed on a train to Switzerland – where they finally regained their freedom. On the journey, Margarete Wiener, whose health had slowly deteriorated over the course of their imprisonment, became too ill to continue travelling. On 25 January 1945, she was taken into a Swiss hospital where she died a few hours later.

Hedwig Brahm

Philipp Manes: journals, portrait and an illustration of the ghetto at Theresienstadt, 1942-1944

Philipp Manes (1875-1944) was a German Jew and a prolific writer with a lifelong habit of keeping records of his experiences. In July 1942, the Nazis deported Manes and his wife to Theresienstadt ghetto. In the ghetto, Manes organised a cultural programme as head of the Orientation Service.

Conditions in the Theresienstadt ghetto, although appalling, were better than those in many other ghettos. This allowed for the creation of extensive cultural and educational programmes. Over 500 lectures were held, organised in part by Philipp Manes. Children received art lessons and orchestras were established. Victor Ullmann and Peter Kien wrote a satirical opera, *The Emperor of Atlantis* (the original libretto of which is in the Library's collections), inside the ghetto.

This is a selection of the large collection of Manes' journals held by The Wiener Holocaust Library. They contain contributions from Manes and others.

Philipp Manes and his wife were murdered in Auschwitz in late 1944. Manes' journals survived and were sent to one of his friends after the war, and then to his family. Philipp Manes' daughter Eve eventually deposited them with The Wiener Library.

Amsterdam met het
echte grote zakenleven
Zou haar wel vele opdrachten
geven.

Dit werk ging goed, leuk
was bovendien
Met Henri veel te kunnen
zien.

Annie Hoek Wallach: *Ha-Ha – Ja-Ja*, c.1943

This book was written and illustrated by Annie Hoek Wallach (b. 1908) and dedicated to her husband, Dr Henri Hoek. Annie was a German Jewish immigrant who lived in the Netherlands during the Nazi era. Her husband, a Dutch Jewish teacher, was deported to a concentration camp where he perished. This book recounts their first meeting and subsequent life together.

Annie Hoek Wallach was born in 1908 in Cologne. In 1933 she decided there was no future for her in Germany, and managed to obtain employment in a textile firm in the Netherlands. In November 1938 she got permission for her mother and sister to emigrate and join her there.

Annie married Dutch Jewish teacher Dr Henri Hoek in February 1942. The couple went into hiding separately in October 1942, Henri in Amsterdam and Annie in Haarlem, but Henri was arrested in April 1943. He was transferred to Westerbork, then deported to Sobibor where he was murdered in May 1943. Annie Hoek Wallach stayed in hiding until the liberation. She later donated this copy of *Ha-Ha Ja-Ja* to The Wiener Holocaust Library.

"UND SIE BEWEGT SICH DOCH!"

FREIE DEUTSCHE DICHTUNG

John Heartfield

John Heartfield: *Freie Deutsche Jugend* ('Free German Youth'): *Und Sie Bewegt Doch! Freie Deutsche Dichtung (And Still it Moves! Free German Poetry)*, 1943

Published in London during the war by a German exile group, this book of anti-fascist verse was designed by John Heartfield and features a foreword by artist Oscar Kokoschka. The Free German Youth were an underground resistance group in Germany, and this publication includes pieces by German anti-Nazi exiles living in Britain, the USA and the Soviet Union, including Berthold Brecht.

The artist John Heartfield (1891-1968) was born Helmut Herzfeld in Berlin. He is particularly known for his production of satirical photomontages featuring anti-Nazi and anti-fascist designs. Herzfeld began to style himself by the English-sounding name John Heartfield during the First World War in protest at the virulent anti-British sentiment he encountered in Berlin. Known as a fierce opponent of Nazism, Heartfield was sought by the Gestapo from shortly after the Nazi accession to power in 1933. He fled on foot to Czechoslovakia. Later, Heartfield came to Britain as a refugee. During the war he was interned as an 'enemy alien', and after the war was refused permission to settle in Britain. Heartfield went to live in East Berlin in 1950.

John Heartfield designed this volume and produced its satirical cover illustration, which depicts Hitler as an ape bestriding the world. Despite Hitler's attempts at world domination, the earth is shown as still spinning on its axis; something that is reflected in the title of the book: *Und Sie Bewegt Doch!* – 'And still it moves!', which is in turn a statement that is supposed to have been made by Galileo Galilei after he was forced by the Inquisition to renounce the idea that the earth is in motion.

The cover of this book is one of a number of copies of satirical anti-Nazi cartoons held by The Wiener Holocaust Library.

Königliche
Schwedische Gesandtschaft
Budapest

Tekintetes

Bródy György urnak

B u d a p e s t.

A Svéd Kir. Követség megbizza

V.Katona József utca 31.számu svéd védett ház <u>házparancsnoki</u>

teendőinek ellátásával.

A Kir.Követség kéri, hogy a ház parancsnoki teendőit

a legnagyobb körültekintéssel, a védettek érdekeinek szem előtt

tartásával ellátni sziveskedjkék.

Ezen megbizásunk visszavonásig érvényes.

Budapest, 1944. december 2-án.

Kir.Svéd Követségi titkár.

Raoul Wallenberg: certificate from the Swedish Embassy in Budapest, 1944

This certificate, issued by the Swedish Embassy in Budapest and signed by Swedish diplomat Raoul Wallenberg (1912-1947), authorised George Brody to act as caretaker for a block of flats which was used by the Swedish Embassy as a safe haven for Hungarian Jews. Brody (1895-1976) was part of a Hungarian-Jewish family who survived in Budapest during the war. This document helped to ensure that Brody was not deported.

After the occupation of Hungary in March 1944, the Swedish delegation there launched a rescue operation to save Jews from being deported. The newly created American War Refugee Board decided to work with the Swedish government, who asked them to send a special envoy to deal with passports.

Raoul Wallenberg was appointed special envoy and arrived in Budapest in July 1944. Here, he saved the lives of thousands of Hungarian Jews by issuing protective passes (*Schutzpass*). Wallenberg disappeared in January 1945 after being taken by Soviet soldiers, and has since been recognised as one of the Righteous Among the Nations, an honorary title given by Israel to recognise non-Jews who aided Jews during the Holocaust.

The document is part of a collection of family papers donated to the Library by the Hungarian-Jewish Brody-Pauncz family in 1986.

KL.: *Weimar Buchenwald* Jude Hollerith erfaßt

Häftlings-Personal-Karte

Fam.-Name: **Pasternák**

Vorname: **Abraham**		**Überstellt**	**Personen-Beschreibung:**
Geb. am: **3.3.24** in: **Bethlen**	am: **6.6.44** an KL.: **Buchenwald**		Grösse: **175** cm
Stand: **led.** Kinder:			Gestalt: **mittelst.**
Wohnort: **Bethlen,Kom.Szolnok Doboka,**	am: an KL.:		Gesicht: **oval**
Strasse: **Zenéez 624**			Augen: **blau**
Religion: **mos.** Staatsang.: **Ungarn**			Nase: **gerade**
Wohnort d. Angehörigen: **Bruder:**	am: an KL.:		Mund: **gew.**
Mendel F.,15/2 KMB,Szkotorszka,			Ohren: **l.absteh.**
UP Valuc,Kom.Bereg	am: an KL.:		Zähne: **2 fehlen**
Eingewiesen am: **30.5.44**			Haare: **rötlish**
durch: **Auschwitz**	am: an KL.:		Sprache: **jidisch,ungar.,**
in KL.:			**rumän.,deutsch,ital.**
Grund: **Polit.Ungar-Jude**			Bes. Kennzeichen: **—**
Vorstrafen:	am: **Entlassung:** durch KL.:		Charakt.-Eigenschaften:

mit Verfügung v.:

Sicherheit b. Einsatz: **I.T.S 857 W**

Strafen im Lager:

Grund:	Art:

Körperliche Verfassung:

U 76 44 1363

Buchenwald Prisoner Card for Ábrahám Paszternák
1.1.5.3/6781448/WHL ITS Archive

This Buchenwald prisoner card for Ábrahám Paszternák is an example of the more than 30 million documents that can be found in The Wiener Holocaust Library's digital copy of the International Tracing Service (ITS) archive (now known as the Arolsen Archives). The ITS holds documentation on some 17.5 million people who were caught up in the Holocaust and the Second World War and its aftermath. It was created to help find missing people and to facilitate family reunions. The Library is the only copyholder and access point to the full digital collection in the United Kingdom.

Born in Bethlen, Hungary (Transylvania) in 1924, Ábrahám Paszternák was one of six children in a religious, Yiddish-speaking family. Between mid-May and early July 1944, Hungarian and German authorities organised the deportation of nearly 440,000 Hungarian Jews. In May 1944, Hungarian gendarmes rounded up Paszternák and his family and herded them into an open-air ghetto. They were then deported by train to Auschwitz-Birkenau. He and two of his brothers survived the 'selection' process, and Paszternák was sent for slave labour to Buchenwald, to a work commando in a brickyard, and then to Schlieben (a subcamp of Buchenwald). From there he was taken to Theresienstadt. After liberation he returned briefly to Hungary and then emigrated to the United States. Ábrahám Paszternák died in Detroit in 2017.

Paszternák's Buchenwald card demonstrates how arbitrary the classification and identification of inmates in the Nazi camp system could be. For example, although Paszternák was arrested and deported from Hungary because he was a Jew, the triangle with a "U" for *Ungar* (Hungarian) appears on the upper right-hand corner of the card. Additionally, although Paszternák was persecuted for being Jewish, the reason (*Grund*) given for his arrest in the left-hand column indicates that he was arrested as a Jewish-Hungarian political offender (*Grund: Polit. Ungar-Jude*). Elsewhere, camp authorities emphasised his Jewish heritage and religion. The single word *Jüde* [sic] is typed across the top of the card, and in the left-hand column, his religion is listed as *mos.*, which is in abbreviation of the German word *mosaisch* (commonly used at the time to refer to Judaism).

The prisoner card also presents important vital information, such as his birth date, last known address, and a physical description. The card includes a photograph, which is infrequent within the ITS archive. The physical description on the right (*Personen-Beschreibung*) includes his height (175 cm); the shape of his face (oval); colour of eyes (blue); colour of his hair (red); the fact that he was missing two teeth, and that he spoke Yiddish, Hungarian, Romanian, German and Italian.

Since 2013, the Library's ITS research support service has helped thousands of people to learn more about persecuted relatives using documents like this.

JEWISH CENTRAL INFORMATION OFFICE
19 Manchester Square,   May, 1945
London, W. 1

Jewish Survivors Report
Documents of Nazi Guilt

No. 1

Eighteen Months

in the

Oswiecim Extermination Camp

By

M. Lichtenstein

This is the first of a series of personal reports
received by the

JEWISH CENTRAL INFORMATION OFFICE

from eye-witnesses of

the persecution of Jews under Nazi rule.

Mordechai Lichtenstein: *Eighteen Months in the Oswiecim Extermination Camp*, 1945

This pamphlet was published by the Jewish Central Information Office (as The Wiener Holocaust Library was then still officially known) in London in 1945. It is one of the earliest accounts produced by a survivor of Auschwitz, and it reflects the JCIO's commitment to gathering and disseminating evidence of the Holocaust. The pamphlet is labelled 'Documents of Nazi Guilt'. The report begins with an account of how it came to be in the collection:

> *One of the few survivors of the horrors of the infamous Nazi concentration camp at Oswiecim (Auschwitz), Poland, paid a visit to our London Institute shortly after he reached Great Britain on the last stage of his recent escape. We have carefully checked our informant's identity and reliability, and are certain that his report is true in every detail.*

The author, Mordechai Lichtenstein, was born in Bendzin, Poland in 1912. In this account, he tells of his own experiences of Nazi persecution, and also provides information about the operation of Auschwitz: Lichtenstein, perhaps at the JCIO's behest, seemed to be consciously seeking to provide historical evidence.

Auschwitz was a camp complex containing slave labour camps, a death camp and a concentration camp. Around 1.1 million people were murdered there, of whom approximately 960,000 were Jews. Between 250,000-300,000 Jews survived Nazi camps and 'death marches' (the Nazis' chaotic and brutal evacuations of prisoners from the camps towards the end of the war), including Mordechai Lichtenstein.

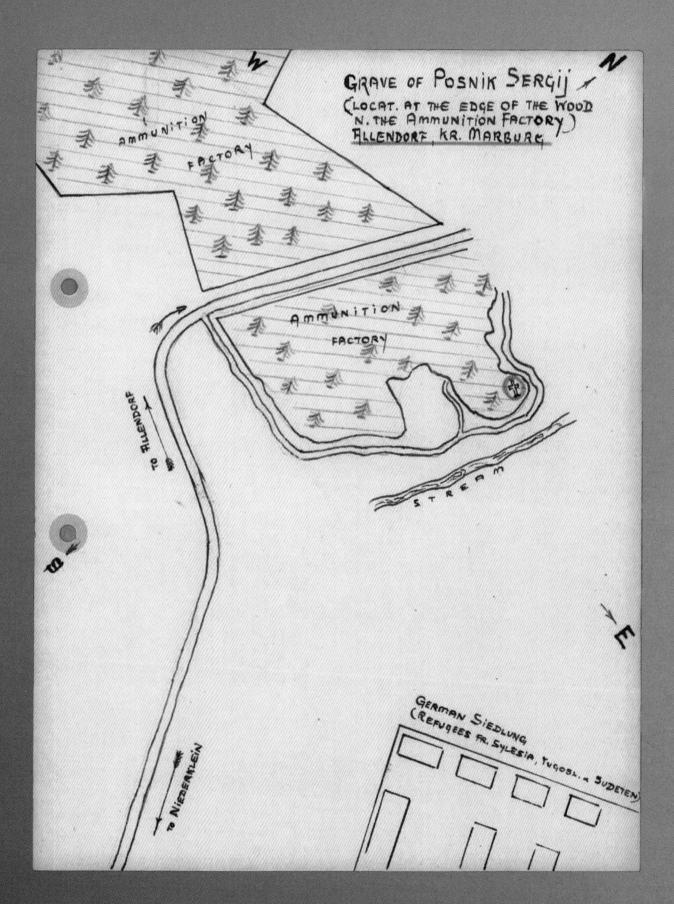

GRAVE OF POSNIK SERGIJ
(LOCAT. AT THE EDGE OF THE WOOD
N. THE AMMUNITION FACTORY)
ALLENDORF, KR. MARBURG

AMMUNITION FACTORY

AMMUNITION FACTORY

STREAM

TO ALLENDORF

TO NIEDERKLEIN

GERMAN SiEDLUNG
(REFUGEES FR. SYLESIA, YUGOSL. & SUDETEN)

Map showing the grave of Sergii Posnik

101100389#1/WHL ITS Archive

In the immediate aftermath of the Second World War, staff at what came to be known as the International Tracing Service (ITS) searched for both the living and the dead. They were tenacious in trying to locate the remains of people who were killed and buried on forced marches. Investigators interviewed witnesses, followed the routes of the marches and exhumed the bodies of those killed. This is one of the maps drawn by them in their search for the body of Sergii Posnik (1926-1945), a prisoner who was killed near Marburg.

Documents like this found in the ITS archive are invaluable to those who continue to search today for information about those who were persecuted during the Holocaust.

The 'Boys' arriving in Windermere, 1945

This image shows some child survivors of the Holocaust disembarking from a plane on their arrival in Britain.

After the end of the Second World War, the British government granted asylum to 1,000 child survivors of the Holocaust. Only 732 survivors could be found and of these the majority were male. As a result, upon arrival in the Lake District in August 1945 the group became collectively known as 'The Boys', despite the presence of around 200 girls.

The boy holding the young child in this photograph is Sidney Finkel (b. 1931), who survived the Piotrków ghetto, a forced labour camp in Poland, Buchenwald concentration camp and a death march to Theresienstadt.

The man receiving the young child is Finkel's older brother Isaac (1914-1992) who survived in ghettos, forced labour camps and Buchenwald. The boy right next to Sidney Finkel (with suitcase in hand) has been identified as Moniek Shannon (1932-2022). He too survived a ghetto, forced labour camp, Buchenwald and a death march to Theresienstadt.

This image comes from the Library's collection of documents relating to the Jewish Committee for Relief Abroad (JCRA), an Anglo-Jewish organisation that supported displaced persons and Holocaust survivors from 1943-1950. The JCRA was funded partly by the Central British Fund for World Jewish Relief, the organisation that managed the rescue of the Windermere children and took responsibility for their welfare once they arrived in Britain.

רחל אויערבאך

אויף די פעלדער
פון
טרעבלינקע

ווארשע - לאדזש - קראקע
1947

Rachel Auerbach: *Oyf di felder fun Treblinka* (*In the Fields of Treblinka*), 1947

Rachel Auerbach (1903-1976) was involved in Emmanuel Ringelblum's underground *Oyneg Shabes* ('Joy of Sabbath') group, who gathered evidence and testimonies in the Warsaw Ghetto. She later worked to document the Holocaust. In this Yiddish-language pamphlet, *In the Fields of Treblinka*, published in 1947, Auerbach revealed early evidence about the extermination camp of Treblinka. The Wiener Holocaust Library holds a copy of this important pamphlet.

Rachel Auerbach was born in the Galician city of Łanowce and in the 1920s studied philosophy and psychology in Lviv. She then moved to Warsaw and worked as a journalist. In the 1940s, as well as working for 'Joy of Sabbath' Auerbach ran a soup kitchen in the Warsaw Ghetto. She managed to escape the ghetto in 1943 and survived in hiding. 'Joy of Sabbath', realising that the Nazi authorities planned to deport all the inhabitants of the ghetto, buried the documents they had amassed.

After the war, Auerbach continued the work of the Ringelblum Archive at the Central Jewish Historical Commission in Poland. She helped to locate parts of the archive from their hiding places and she also gathered survivor reports. In 1950, she emigrated to Israel where she led the Yad Vashem Eyewitness Accounts Department. In 1960-61, Rachel Auerbach supported the preparations for the trial of Adolf Eichmann and testified in court against him.

Unzer Sztyme (*Our Voice*), 1949

This Yiddish language and Zionist periodical was published in the Bergen-Belsen
Displaced Persons (DP) camp after the Second World War. Belsen, which had been a
Nazi concentration camp, was administered by as part of the British zone of occupation
following its liberation. It became the largest Jewish DP camp in Germany.

There were hundreds of camps for so-called DPs in occupied Germany, but mostly in
the British and American Zones. The camps became a temporary home for Jewish
survivors, who established their own administrations, schools, and even a football
league. The last camp closed in 1957.

Initially, many camps had their own newsletter. With time, and as the many camps
were consolidated, the newsletters of the larger camps, such as *Unzer Sztyme* – 'Our
Voice', were the most widely read. Eventually, *Unzer Sztyme* became the main
newspaper read by Jewish DPs in the British zone of occupation. This partly reflected
the support that Jewish DPs had for Zionism in the aftermath of the Holocaust and also
Belsen's role as a site where Jewish life and culture was re-established after the war.
Unzer Sztyme also dealt with matters of Jewish faith, as can be seen on the cover of this
volume, where a Shofar – a horn used in Jewish religious observance – is depicted
being blown.

Alfred Wiener in London, 1950s

The Director of The Wiener Holocaust Library, Alfred Wiener, is pictured here at his desk in the Library's then-headquarters at Manchester Square, central London, in the 1950s. The Library, still called the JCIO, had opened in Manchester Square on 1 September 1939.

During the war, the JCIO was increasingly referred to as Dr Wiener's Library and was largely funded by the British government as it was recognised, at least early on in the war, as the leading source of information about the Nazi movement in Britain. During the war, the JCIO collected evidence of the persecution and later mass murder of Jews in Nazi Germany and German-occupied Europe. It also continued to gather Nazi publications. After the war, Alfred Wiener continued to promote the JCIO/Wiener Library mission of monitoring and analysing antisemitism. Over time, the organisation became a historical institute, dedicated to gathering and disseminating evidence about the Holocaust.

Alfred Wiener resigned as Director of the Library in 1961, aged 75. He died in 1964.

Eva Reichmann photographed in London, 1952

This photograph shows Dr Eva Reichmann (1897-1998) at work in The Wiener Library in Manchester Square. Reichmann was at this time the Director of Research at the Library, where she led an ambitious project to collect and record eyewitness accounts of the Holocaust from across Europe. Over a period of seven years, and with financial support from The Conference on Jewish Material Claims Against Germany, Reichmann and her team gathered reports from refugees, survivors and others, in Britain and abroad. The project amassed more than 1,300 reports in seven different languages.

Reichmann was born in 1897 in Upper Silesia, and earned a DPhil in economics in 1921. She married lawyer and activist Hans Reichmann in 1932. Reichmann became an advisor to the Central Association of German Citizens of Jewish Faith. Following Hans Reichmann's release from Sachsenhausen after the events of *Kristallnacht*, the couple emigrated to Britain in 1939. Eva Reichmann's research on Nazi antisemitism was published in 1950 as *Hostages of Civilisation*. From 1942-1943, Reichmann worked for the BBC's German listening service, after which she became the Director of Research at The Wiener Library.

The eyewitness accounts remain an important part of the Library's collections. Many of them are now translated into English and available online for new generations of Holocaust researchers: www.testifyingtothetruth.co.uk

SLAVE WORKER

by JOHN DALMAU

1'-

in the CHANNEL ISLANDS

John Dalmau: *Slave Worker in the Channel Islands,* 1956

The author of this pamphlet, John Dalmau (dates unknown), was a Republican soldier of the Spanish Civil War who had joined the French Army and was subsequently taken captive by the Germans in 1940. He was forced to work on the construction of the Atlantic Wall in northern France, and then sent to work in Jersey and Alderney, where he witnessed horrific brutality and the starvation of prisoners. In 1943, Dalmau was involved in the sabotage of a German vessel. After the war, Dalmau settled in Guernsey and had a family.

During the German occupation of the Channel Islands of 1940-1945, many thousands of people were persecuted, including slave labourers, political prisoners and Jews. As the defeated British and French armies evacuated from Dunkirk in May and June 1940, British authorities decided not to defend the Channel Islands. The Islands were demilitarised and 25 percent of the residents remained behind. Germany invaded in late June-early July 1940.

The German occupiers made extensive use of foreign labourers in the Channel Islands. A minority of the workers were volunteers, while others were forced labourers, who received wages, or slaves, who did not. Labourers included Soviet citizens, Eastern Europeans, Spaniards, French citizens, North Africans, Dutch, and Belgians. The workers all suffered from maltreatment, including brutal beatings and a lack of food, but Jews and Soviet citizens were especially badly treated. Some slave workers were murdered.

Labourers were engaged in construction projects, primarily the fortification of the Islands as part of the Atlantic Wall scheme. All worked for *Organisation Todt* (OT), the Nazi engineering and construction organisation. At its peak, 16,000 OT labourers were based in the Islands.

In excess of 1,000 foreign forced and slave labourers died in the Channel Islands during the occupation, mainly from maltreatment. Between 437 and 1,000 predominately Soviet citizens died in Alderney alone.

On 9 May 1945, the Channel Islands became the last place to be liberated from Nazi occupation.

P.III.g. No. 518

Bericht über die Widerstandsgruppe Herbert Baum in Berlin.

Etwa in den Jahren 1938/39 schlossen sich mehrere junge jüdische Genossen zu einer Widerstandsgruppe zusammen. Sie kamen meist aus dem Mittelstand und waren aus der jüdischen Jugendbewegung verschiedener Richtung hervorgegangen. Schon dort hatte man sich mit der Theorie des Sozialismus beschäftigt. Fast alle waren Facharbeiter geworden und waren schon vor 1933 dem Kommunistischen Jugendverband oder der Kom. Partei Deutschlands beigetreten. Auch hatten einige unserer Kameraden bereits mit den Gefängnissen Hitlerdeutschlands Bekanntschaft gemacht. der Kern der Gruppe bestand aus Herbert Baum und seiner Frau Marianne. Herbert Baum hatte sein Ingenieurstudium abbrechen müssen durch den Nazismus und war nun Mechaniker. Er hatte ein gutes politisches Wissen war zäh und geschickt bei der Arbeit und seinem Elan verdankt die Gruppe zum Teil ihren starken Zusammenhalt.

Zur Gruppe gehörten ferner Felix Heymann, Alfred Eisenstädter, Gert und Hanny Meyer, Heinz Birnbaum, Irene Walter und Suzanne Wesse, eine Französin, die nach Berlin geheiratet hatte. Später kamen noch Richard Holzer, Hella und Alice Hirsch, Heinz Rotholz, Charlotte Paech spätere Holzer, und Edith Fränkel zur Gruppe Baum. Hatte der engere Kreis schon seit Jahren enge persönliche Beziehungen, so waren die Anderen dazu gekommen, um aus der Isolierung durch den Faschismus herauszukommen.

Die Gruppe versuchte nun, durch gemeinsame Wanderungen, Musik- und Leseabende ihre innere Kraft aufrecht zu erhalten, nicht in Lethargie gegenüber dem jüdischen Schicksal zu verfallen. Zugleich aber wurde unter der Leitung von Herbert Baum eine systematische Schulungsarbeit betrieben, die sich auf die wenige erreichbare Marxistische Literatur stützte und das Ziel hatte, der Gruppe das Rüstzeug für die illegale Arbeit zu geben.

So entstand allmählig eine Widerstandsgruppe, die sich Aufgaben stellen konnte. Zunächst wurden Verbindungen mit anderen Widerstands- gruppen aufgenommen, um Kontakt mit der illegalen KPD zu haben und dadurch Informationen und Anweisungen zu erhalten.

Jeder Einzelne unserer Gruppe begann nun an seiner Arbeitsstelle unter den jüdischen Zwangsarbeitern, aber auch unter den anderen Arbeitern Mut zuzusprechen und zu warnen, dass man nicht allem zusehen darf, sondern gemeinsam mit allen Antifaschisten den Kampf gegen den Nazismus aufnehmen muss.

Bald wurde der Einfluss der Gruppe Baum spürbar, besonders in der Zwangsarbeitergruppe bei Siemens, wo die Meisten Mitglieder der Baum- gruppe arbeiteten. Anfang des Jahres 1941 konnte eine weitere Gruppe jüdischer Jugendlicher, die sich bei Siemens zusammengefunden hatten, zur Mitarbeit herangezogen werden. Der Leiter dieser Gruppe war Heinz Joachim, ein sehr begabter Musiker und seine Frau Marianne. Zu diesem

Richard and Charlotte Holzer: report of the Baum Group's activities, 1957

This is a document from the Eyewitness Accounts collection of The Wiener Holocaust Library. Charlotte Holzer, née Abraham (1909-1980), was sentenced to death in 1943 for her role in the Baum Group, an anti-Nazi resistance group in Berlin, but managed to escape from a prison hospital in 1944. Charlotte and Richard Holzer (1911-1975) married after the war and lived in East Germany. Charlotte Holzer campaigned for recognition of the memory of the Baum Group.

Herbert Baum, his wife and some of their friends formed an anti-Nazi resistance group in Berlin in the 1930s. Almost all members of the group were Jewish. Initially, the Baum Group were motivated primarily by their communist beliefs. From 1936, they also increasingly resisted because of their opposition to the Nazis' persecution of Jews. In 1940, after Baum was forced to work at a Siemens plant in the city, he recruited other mainly young Jewish forced labourers to the group, and it expanded to around 100 members.

At the time of the German invasion of the Soviet Union in 1941, the group distributed leaflets publicising the brutality and atrocities of the invasion. On 18 May 1942, they carried out an arson attack on an anti-communist and antisemitic Nazi exhibition called *Soviet Paradise*. Most of those involved in the bombing were arrested and executed. Herbert Baum was probably murdered in Moabit Prison on 11 June 1942.

Mannswörth ist ein langgestrecktes Dorf in der Nähe von Schwechat
in Niederösterreich. Die Landschaft trägt schon den Charakter der
Tiefebene und man ahnt die ungarische Puszta. Hier wohnt Frau
Hermine Horvath, der unser Besuch gilt.

Bald haben wir das Haus Nr. 186 gefunden. Für Frau Horvath völlig
überraschend, klopfen wir an ihre Tür.

Eine junge Frau steht in der Küche. Kurze, braune Stiefel, Ski-
hose und ein buntes Kopftuch nach unten gebunden. Das Gesicht,
die Augen wirken jung. Nicht zu glauben, dass diese Frau schon
die Hölle von Auschwitz-Birkenau hinter sich hat und doch ist es
so.

Frau Horvath ist sich unschlüssig, was sie tun soll, als wir so
plötzlich an ihr vergangenes Leben pochen. Man merkt, wie viele
Fragen durch ihr Hirn jagen. Wird sie sich verschliessen, sollten
wir umsonst gekommen sein. Den Vorschlag, dass wir in zwei Stunden
nochmals kommen, nimmt sie gern an.

Als wir dann eintreten, sitzt sie auf einem Sofa und schreibt eifrig
in einem Heft. Sie möchte ihre Gedanken ordnen und sie uns dann
gleich aufgeschrieben mitgeben. Es ist noch eine Kluft zwischen ihr
und uns. Hinter diesem Heftchen will sie sich wohl verschanzen.
In 5 Minuten wird es klarer. Sie verlangt einen Ausweis, den wir
ihr gerne zeigen und bald schmilzt das Eis des Misstrauens in der
Wärme des gegenseitigen Verstehens. Denn das dass, was in Auschwitz-
Birkenau geschah, niemals vergessen werde, ist ihr heisser Wunsch.

Wir versuchen nun das wiederzugeben, was Frau Horvath erzählte:

Meine Eltern waren sesshafte Zigeuner. Unsere Heimat war Jabing in
Südburgenland (Österreich). Mein Vater war Spengler. Er kam weit
herum. Wir hatten ein Häuschen und auch einen Weingarten und einen
Flecken Wald. Im Sommer arbeitete mein Vater noch in der Landwirt-
schaft. So wurde eifrigst gespart, damit wir sechs Kinder nicht zu
hungern brauchten.

Mit dem Einmarsch der deutschen Truppen im Frühling 1938 wurde alles
anders. Da brach für uns eine schlimme Zeit an.

Wir waren in allem rechtlos. Wir durften die Schule nicht mehr besuchen. Wir durften nur in der Zeit von 11-12 Uhr einkaufen. Wir
durften keine Tanzveranstaltung, kein Kino, keine öffentliche Ver-
anstaltung besuchen, kurz: wir waren Ausgestossene. Damals war
ich 13. Jahre alt und meine Mutter erwartete das 7. Kind.

Hermine Horvath: eyewitness account of sexual abuse, 1958

In 1958 in Vienna, as part of The Wiener Library's efforts to gather eyewitness accounts of the Holocaust, a Wiener Library researcher interviewed Hermine Horvath (c.1924-1958), a Roma woman originally from Burgenland in Austria. This is a rare example of a testimony by a Romani survivor from this time. Unusually for an account taken during this period, Horvath was very candid about the sexual abuse she experienced and witnessed at the hands of the SS.

In this document, Horvath describes the situation for her family after the German takeover of Austria in March 1938. Her father was deported to Dachau concentration camp in June 1938. Horvath also speaks of one occasion in Austria in the late 1930s, when an SS man on whose farm she was a forced labourer threatened her:

> *I noticed very quickly that this* [local SS leader] *did not worry at all about the Racial Problem when it came to a young Gypsy girl. He started to come after me... One day he was suddenly standing in front of me with a drawn pistol.*

Horvath fought him off and informed his wife of his actions.

Later, following her deportation to Auschwitz-Birkenau in 1943, Horvath recounts how she witnessed the rape and murder of two Romani children by an SS officer in Auschwitz.

Hermine Horvath died at 33, shortly after her testimony was given, likely as a result of the privations she had suffered as a camp inmate, slave labourer and victim of forced experimentation.

Reimar Gilsenbach: photograph of Margarete Kraus, 1960s

Journalist Reimar Gilsenbach (1925-2001) interviewed Margarete Kraus (1928-2005) about her experiences of persecution in Ludwigslust in East Germany in 1966. This photograph is likely to date from then. In the photograph, Kraus' Auschwitz camp number is visible, tattooed on her left forearm.

Kraus, originally from Czechoslovakia, was deported with her family to Auschwitz in about 1943 when she was a teenager. There they were held in the *Zigeunerfamilienlager*, the 'Gypsy family camp'. In Auschwitz, Kraus experienced maltreatment and privation, and contracted typhus. She was also subject to forced medical experiments. Kraus' parents died in Auschwitz and Kraus was later transferred to Ravensbrück concentration camp.

This photograph may have come into the Library's collections as part of the Kenrick Collection, a set of documents collected by Donald Kenrick and Grattan Puxon in the 1960s as part of their research into the genocide against Europe's Roma. Their project was the first attempt to comprehensively document the genocide, and it was part-funded by The Wiener Library.

Drawings by child survivors of genocide, Darfur 2007

This is one of over 500 drawings donated to the Library in 2014 by Waging Peace, a human rights organisation that campaigns against genocide and human rights abuses in Sudan and supports Sudanese refugees to Britain. The drawings were made by child survivors of the genocide perpetrated, from 2003, by deposed President Omar al Bashir's Sudanese government forces and the *Janjaweed* militia against non-Arab Darfuri people. They were collected by an anonymous Waging Peace researcher in June and July 2007.

When the researcher was collecting testimonies from adults, the women described how their children had witnessed horrendous sights when villages were attacked by government forces and *Janjaweed* militia. In response, the researcher gave children aged six to eighteen pen and paper and asked them to draw what they remembered. The drawings include depictions of adult men and women being shot, beaten and taken prisoner; babies being thrown onto fires, and the looting and burning of villages.

In 2009, the International Criminal Court accepted many of these drawings as contextual evidence of the crimes committed in Darfur. The pattern of the attacks shown in these drawings corroborates other evidence of the attacks in Darfur and contradicts the account given by the Government of Sudan to the ICC. In 2019, The Wiener Holocaust Library accepted a further donation of drawings by children who have faced persecution by Sudanese government forces in the Nuba Mountains in Southern Sudan, along with petitions produced in refugee camps in Darfur calling for the prosecution of the perpetrators of human rights violations, and eyewitness testimonies from adults who experienced the violence in Darfur.

Dr Hartwig Fischer was born in Hamburg in 1962. He is an art historian, a former curator of 19th-century and modern art at the Kunstmuseum Basel and Director of the Folkwang Museum in Essen. He was Director General of the Dresden State Art Collections and, since April 2016, he has been Director of the British Museum.

Dr Barbara Warnock is the Senior Curator and Head of Education at The Wiener Holocaust Library, where she has curated the exhibitions *Jewish Resistance to the Holocaust, Berlin-London*; *The Lost Photographs of Gerty Simon;* and *Forgotten Victims: The Nazi Genocide of the Roma and Sinti*, amongst others. She is the author (with John March) of *Berlin-London: The Lost Photographs of Gerty Simon* (2019), a *Spectator* Book of the Year, and a number of articles on refugee history and the Nazi persecution of Roma.

The Wiener Holocaust Library

The Wiener Holocaust Library is a registered charity and we rely on our friends and supporters to continue and develop our vital work. If you would like to help us to continue our work, then please consider visiting our website to make a donation today.

https://wienerholocaustlibrary.org/what-we-do/support-our-work/donate/